THE LIGHT JEWISH
COOKBOOK

THE LIGHT JEWISH COOKBOOK

Recipes from around the world
for weight loss and health

**SYLVIE JOUFFA AND
ANNICK CHAMPETIER DE RIBES**

translated from the French by Tamsin Black

SOUVENIR PRESS

SUMMARY

VEGETABLES AND SIDE DISHES

PART III
WEIGHT-LOSS DIET
By Annick Champetier de Ribes

PART 1

By Sylvie Jouffa

MY STORY

"I remember those years of living with my grandmother. She was a marvellous cook. I was her pet grandchild and she made the most delicious cookies I've ever tasted and stuffed cabbage and kreplach (pieces of dough, pinched at the corners, stuffed with cheese). I've never tasted those dishes anywhere in the world to match hers."[1]

Lauren Bacall

My story is that of the daughter of Polish Jewish immigrants who fled poverty and the pogroms to seek refuge in France in the early 1930s.

My paternal grandmother, Esther, played mother to the whole family. A former baker and pastry cook in Warsaw, she had spent fifty years at her coal stove in France. As a little girl with my hair in Shirley Temple ringlets, I was thus steeped in the smell of plaited brioche with poppy seeds, cinnamon apple strudel and croissants with yogurt and raisins.

To this day, I have only to shut my eyes to sense these power-ful aromas deep down inside.

A child of the baby boom, I was born in 1945. My mother Régine (Ronia) had just learnt that her whole family, four broth-ers and a sister aged between 12 and 30, her father, aunt and others, had perished in the Warsaw ghetto or in the extermination camps. All, except one sister: my Aunt Annette (Hannah), a champion cheesecake maker, who had come to join her in France

1 Lauren Bacall, *By Myself*, Alfred A. Knopf, 1978.

in 1938. As you can imagine, the atmosphere that surrounded me in my tender youth was anything but cheerful.

After years of 'hide-and-seek war' with the collaborators, the militia, the French police and the German Nazis, my parents went back to their dressmaking business. Like my grandfather Herschel before him, my father Nathan was an excellent tailor. Meanwhile my mother, once an apprentice embroiderer in Warsaw and my father's childhood sweetheart whom he had brought to Paris in 1934, was press-ganged into working as a finisher in the family atelier.

In my earliest years, my parents, who worked hard, left me in the care of my grandmother. I spent my days in her enchanted kitchen, where marvellous dishes were concocted and which served as a kind of tearoom for her friends. The place was a thoroughfare, where friends met and exchanged news; it was also where horrific tales were told by those returning from the camps.

Maurice (Moïshe), my father's brother, had spent several years interned in Auschwitz. He had survived because he had been part of a unit that carted dead bodies from the gas chambers to the crematoria. He had come back slightly crazed. I remember him taking me in his arms and throwing me up in the air, shouting 'bang! bang!'. It was his way of explaining that the Nazis in Auschwitz used to stage 'pigeon shoots,' using children like me. I was terrified.

I was soon given to understand that I was different from other children of my age: I was Jewish, and we lived surrounded by wicked *Goyim* (non-Jews), who hated us and wanted to kill us, and the sooner I knew how things stood the better, on the grounds that forewarned was forearmed. In particular, my mother told me: 'If anyone asks you whether you're Jewish, tell them no. Just tell them you're Protestant and that you come from the Alsace.' Our surnames, Roterman on my father's side, Heldman on my mother's, were of German origin. Yet I wanted to resemble my school friends and be a real French girl.

My grandmother, who could neither read nor write, spoke Yiddish to me. I understood everything but refused to speak any language other than French. So she talked Yiddish and I replied in French, and we understood each other perfectly.

Her friends, whom she often invited in for a cup of tea and an assortment of pastries, would sit and tell her about their war experiences and give her news of this or that person, often someone who had died. She little suspected I understood everything they said.

I thus overheard the most horrendous stories, in spite of which, my grandmother's kitchen provided a sanctuary that sheltered me from the outside world her guests depicted as so inimical, and I felt protected.

Then I grew up and left my gingerbread grandmother. For her part, she grew gradually older, and one day, she left us forever. After her death, I realised that she had taken her culinary treasures with her. It was the end of a whole culture.

At that time, I did not know how to cook, not even spaghetti, but I set out to find her recipes, first from other women in the family, then from her friends and old friends of old friends, and finally from other women from other countries.

One day, I went to interview a lady, who called over her aged mother, a woman of ninety and barely able to walk. I trembled with excitement when, from a drawer, she produced a notebook yellowed with age and gave me one of her grandmother's recipes. It had been written in the mid-nineteenth century and for me was like gold-dust for all it was nothing more than an onion pancake!

After collecting recipes from Eastern Europe, I gathered others from North Africa and Asia from more old ladies, most of whom are now dead. They are original and authentic recipes, passed down from generation to generation since the dawn of time.

I spent my childhood hiding the fact that I was Jewish and developed quite a complex about not being a real Catholic French girl like most of my friends at a Parisian elementary school in the Rue de Marseille, near the Saint-Martin Canal.

Over time, I understood that I belonged to a brave people, who have never abandoned the fight to preserve their cultural, religious and culinary traditions.

By writing and publishing Jewish recipe books, I have found fulfilment and learnt finally and fearlessly to be proud of my origins.

My books are intended for women who, like myself, are

searching for their roots and hoping to discover the flavors of their childhood.

They are also for younger generations from any background, who are looking for innovative dishes.

MY DIET

How I lost weight efficiently and without stress

When I met the dietician Annick Champetier de Ribes, I had too much cholesterol and was showing signs of high blood pressure. My GP strongly recommended I think about going on a diet.

Six months later and nine kilos lighter, my cholesterol had totally disappeared and my blood pressure was back to normal.

Throughout the diet Annick suggested, I never felt frustrated or duty-bound. From the outset, I was allowed one day off a week, when I could eat what I liked.

I made sure I was organised and adopted a healthy routine, fitting in twenty minutes' exercise each morning between breakfast and my shower.

The years dropped away with the dress sizes (I lost two), and I treated myself to a whole new wardrobe. My friends and my husband and children thought I looked better and blooming. I had tried many of the latest diets, all without lasting success, and was sceptical at the start, but now I felt good about myself. At sixty, I had succeeded in going back to the weight I had been at 20.

Annick Champetier de Ribes was a precious guide, 'a coach', in modern-day parlance. Thanks to a diet and advice tailored to my needs and personality, I lost weight efficiently with none of the side-effects of tiredness or stress. I am currently in a stabilising phase and am allowed three days off per week. That means that every other day, I can eat anything I like (within limits, of course) at one of the two main meals: piece of chocolate now and then, a cake, the odd ice-cream. Not bad, eh?

For six months, every day, I entered on to my computer everything I ate for breakfast, lunch and dinner. That might seem time-consuming, but it's essential to keep tabs on yourself.

With an electrode strapped to one foot and attached to a medical monitor, the dietician measured how much fat, muscle and water I had. She was then able to work out what my personal diet should be. Then she gave me a photocopy of a book with, on one page, an *example of food distribution for a day*, which I had to follow for six days of the week. As I had too much fat, I was recommended to go on a diet that consisted of protein (dairy products, lean meat and fish) at each meal. It also included green vegetables, soup, raw vegetables, fruit and also bread and starch in specific quantities with a little fat, oil or margarine.

The guide went on to explain my *blood-fat reducing, low-calorie diet*: for example, how to increase my energy output by being physically active; how to reduce cholesterol by eating fish three or four times a week, replacing animal fats with vegetable fats and eating green and raw vegetables.

Then came a page of *tips to help me in my diet*: no nibbling between meals, chew your food thoroughly and eat large quantities of raw and cooked vegetables at every meal in order to feel full.

The guide also included a three-page list of *protein equivalents* so that I could vary my diet. For instance, 100g meat = 2 eggs = 100g fish = 300g × 20% yogurt. Or 30g 45% fat cheese = 50g cold meat = 60g 30% fat cheese.

Then there were *carbohydrate equivalents*: 40g bread can be replaced by 100g potatoes or 100g cooked rice or cooked pasta.

Fruit equivalents: 1 apple = 3 apricots = 2 kiwis = 200 ml orange juice (without added sugar) = 200g strawberries, etc.

Fat equivalents: 10g fat = 10g butter or margarine (a knob) = 1 tablespoon oil, etc.

Examples of calorie equivalents: 10g fat = 1 glass (100 ml) wine = 40g bread, etc.

The book also suggested a list of foods of which you can *as much as you like*. It included all green vegetables, lettuce, cabbage, mushrooms, tomatoes, runner beans, and so on, followed by examples of healthy salads.

A table with the title *choice of foods* described the food groups: dairy products; meat; fish; eggs; starch; sweetened foods; fruit; green vegetables, fat and drinks. For each group, there was food that was permitted and food that was not recommended. Among the drinks, for example, still or sparkling water, flavoured water without added sugar, tea, coffee, herbal teas and vegetable broth were all permitted. Those not recommended included sweetened drinks, lemonade, Coca Cola and fizzy drinks generally, fruit squash, alcohol, aperitifs, liqueurs, beer, cider, and so on.

A page of *cook's tips* gave the different types of cooking (baking, grilling or steaming, for example) to avoid frying. These culinary tips were followed by suggestions for reducing the fat in certain dishes.

The last two pages provided varied *examples of menus*, from day 1 to day 16 at the start of the diet.

Thanks to these written recommendations, which I followed to the letter, I enjoyed a balanced and varied diet, I never for an instant felt hungry and I lost weight steadily and free of stress.

I see Annick Champetier de Ribes every month with my own list of daily menus. She analyses them at every session and offers me the wisdom of her counsel and guidance.

When I gave her one of my Jewish cook books, she was interested in the unusual recipes I had spent decades patiently accumulating. She did, however, find them high in calories, which is putting it mildly!

So I then wanted to work with her on a new collection of Jewish recipes. The (justly considered) rich and fatty traditional cuisine must be analysed and transformed by the dietician. Annick Champetier de Ribes agreed, and the project began.

Most of the recipes in this book have therefore been modified to give them a lower fat and sugar content. In some cases, they have been left as they are but are combined with other, lighter dishes to redress the calorie balance. Alongside each recipe, you will find the number of calories it contains, as well as nutritional advice and suggestions for other courses at the same meal.

We also thought about holiday menus, for both Sephardim and Ashkenazim. The dietary prohibitions of the Jewish religion (keeping meat and dairy products separate, for example) are properly respected.

We hope to help you lose weight or stay slim by cooking dishes both classic and rare – and above all by eating good Jewish food without gaining an ounce!

KASHRUT

Nutrition, diet, tradition and religion

Some traditional dishes are dictated by religious festivals, others have become tradition over time. Jewish cooking is thus the result of custom as much as duty.

Holiday meals consist of a whole series of dishes which rarely stem from religious duties, even though they are vaguely linked to the rituals of the holiday in these celebrations. Although on the Sabbath, for example, different dishes are eaten from the rest of the week, this is only because cooking is prohibited on that day. Either you eat cold leftovers cooked the previous day, or you eat food cooked slowly over night on a ring or hearth. In this case, it is true to say that religion has a direct influence on the meal. East European Jews, for instance, eat *cholent*[2], a stew of beans, meat and potatoes that simmers all night on the hob. North African Jews prefer the *tafina* or *dafina*, a different recipe although also based on potatoes and beans.

Each festival has its customs and traditions. Purim, for instance, is a festival when edible presents are given to children and special cakes are baked with cumin filling, called *Haman Pockets* or *Haman Ears*. Why? The story goes that, in the sixth century BC, the favourite minister of Ahasuerus, King of the Persians, had ordered the Jews to be massacred, but they were

---

2 Cholent, from the old French 'chaud lent' or 'slow hot', is a dish which, according to Rabbi Rami Shapiro, was invented by the Jews of northern France (*Contes hasidiques*, Albin Michel, 2007).

saved by Queen Esther. The minister's name was Haman and his ears had 'flown to the wind' ('volé au vent', hence 'vol-au-vent') when he was hanged. Or again: during Pesach or Passover, we make *knaidelach*, a kind of dumpling, because eating bread or pasta is forbidden. Passover (Jewish 'Easter') commemorates the flight of the Hebrews out of Egypt. To recall the bread the Jews hastily baked without leaven before their departure, all yeast-based food is prohibited for eight days. *Knaidelach* are easy to make from matzo meal. At Passover, we also eat dishes flavoured with bitter herbs to symbolise the bitterness of slavery. By contrast, at Sukkot (Pentecost), priority is given to dishes involving milk and honey to represent sweetness at the Ceremony of Bikkurim with its offerings of the first fruits of spring.

In the same way that non-Jews eat turkey at Christmas (although it is not mentioned in the Gospels and no one is considered a bad Christian for eating something else), Jews are under no religious obligation to eat certain dishes. If they do, it is out of respect for tradition.

Ashkenazim, for instance, eat stuffed carp not only because carp is a fish with fins and scales and as such accepted by religion, but mostly because carp is very common in Polish and Russian markets and affordable to poor Jews in the *shtetl*. Nowadays, Jews from Eastern Europe continue to eat carp (mostly on Friday evening to begin the holiday), but only because they love it and not from religious observance.

It is impossible to give Biblical significance to the way Jews eat. There is, of course, no trace of the way they ate in the Ancient World, with the exception of matzos. Jewish cooking from Russia and Poland is similar to that of the Russians and Poles, apart from a few details. The Jews from North Africa eat very similar food to Muslims from the same countries. For a Jewish cook with Moroccan roots, the recipes in a Moroccan cook book will recall the dishes and flavours of her childhood.

While Jewish gastronomy has altered down the ages according to the countries the Jews crossed, by choice or force, and while it borrows ingredients from all these lands, it remains the cuisine of a people united around several religious dictates. Although the Jewish community dispersed throughout the Mediterranean Basin and Central and Eastern Europe over 1,500 years and is now present on every continent, it has managed to retain its identity by avoiding assimilation with *Goyim* (non-Jews) thanks to strict culinary rules. Since total integration was not desirable and was difficult if not impossible to maintain, the children of Israel have survived until the present time as a people, despite secular persecution.

Kashrut is a way of life considered sacred and has been essential in cementing the Diaspora around ritual. To be edible, a dish must be *kosher*, a Hebrew adjective that means 'fit for consumption' for a Jew.

The Bible (Lev. 11, Deut. 14) divides animals into three categories: those on the ground, those that fly and those that swim.

Clean animals that live on the ground are ruminant mammals with cloven hoofs. Clean animals are thus cows, calves, sheep, lambs and goats. Unclean animals are horses, rabbits and pigs.

In Leviticus, we read: '[. . .] *The hare, for it ruminates and does not have a cloven hoof, is unclean for you; the pig, for it has a cloven hoof but does not ruminate, is unclean for you.*' (Torah, Deuteronomy, Chapter XIV, 8).

Pigs seem to be creation's most unclean animal. Archaeologists studying what they believe to be the earliest Israelite homes in the Holy Land east of today's West Bank uncovered the bones of a number of animals, all apart from pigs, which proves how old this food prohibition is, since the villages in the study dated from the 11th and 12th centuries BC.

For flying animals, the Bible gives a list of forbidden birds, including all birds of prey. Tradition, however, is more practical for a nomadic people, and considers that birds consumed in the country where the Jews are staying are clean. Fowl, including chicken, duck, goose, turkey and guinea fowl are clean. Interpretations divide over ostrich, which is a-typical. For animals that live in water, those that are clean have fins and scales. Clean fish include salmon, cod, herring, sardines, whiting, bream, bass, sole, tuna, carp, and so on. Unclean fish include monkfish, skate, eel and all shellfish (prawns, crayfish, lobster, oysters, mussels, etc).

Some insects with wings are basically kosher, but as it is no longer customary to eat them, except in Africa or Asian, they are now considered unclean. Thus, grasshoppers, still eaten by some people in the southern Mediterranean Basin, were once considered clean but have become unclean over time.

If the first rule is not to eat unclean animals, the second (Deut. 12-14, transcribed in Michna, a collection of oral laws from the Babylonian period) is not to eat blood. Blood symbolises the soul, so the flesh of an animal may be eaten but not its soul: '*Only be sure that you do not eat the blood, for the blood is the life, and you may not eat the life with the blood*'.

Ritual slaughter, known as Shechita, which was performed in the Temple by priests in ancient times, consists of slitting the animal's throat with a single blow and allowing the blood to drain out. The meat must then be salted and soaked or broiled so that no blood remains.

The Talmud describes the sacred rites involved in the slaughter of animals, including the shape and length of the knife; severing the animal's carotid and oesophagus; the blessing; examining the entrails to check the animal's state of health; extracting the blood vessels and fat, and rinsing then salting the meat.

Not eating blood necessarily means not eating hunted quarry, since the animal has not been ritually killed. But live animals may be trapped then killed according to the rules.

On the other hand, the animal's hind quarters are not used, in reference to Jacob's sciatic nerve which the Angel damaged (Gen., 32: 26 and ff). Thus, when eating steak, you cannot eat the sirloin.

The third rule, briefly mentioned in the Bible (Ex. 23, 19) is not to mix meat and dairy. It is described as follows: '*You will not boil a kid in its mother's milk.*' Hence the Jewish tradition of not combining milk and meat at the same meal, and this goes for both cooking and eating. So, for instance, you cannot cook an *escalope normande* (involving a rich cream sauce) or a *poulet basquaise à la crème* (mildly spicy chicken with cream). Nor can you follow the French pattern at mealtimes and serve Camembert after a steak, or strawberries and cream after Moroccan couscous with lamb. Traditionally, you should use separate utensils and crockery for dairy and meat to avoid mixing forbidden foods.

Jews must wait several hours before drinking milk after they have eaten meat: six for Sephardim and four for Ashkenazim.

They also have to wait four hours to eat meat after drinking milk. This represents the time it takes to digest so as not to mix dairy and meat in the stomach. If you are at a cocktail party and eating standing up, the French Consistory (the Jewish authority set up by Napoleon and recognised by the Minister of the Interior) advises rinsing your mouth if you have eaten a piece of cheese quiche and are about to attack a meat drumstick.

However, one meat product can hide another! Be careful of chipped and sautéed potatoes, which may have been cooked in animal oil and therefore become *'fleischig'* (containing meat). You also have to look out for soft, processed sweets or those with additives and colourings beloved by children, because they have often been made from gelatine based on bone meal.

Processed food is only kosher if it is produced under the supervision of a religious authority that issues a certificate to say that the rules have been properly observed at all stages of production. This makes kosher products marginally more expensive than non-kosher ones.

Kosher wine is the same as ordinary wine, although the Bible forbids its consumption because it was invented to celebrate the cult of idols. To be kosher, wine must therefore be made without the intervention of *Goyim* (non-Jews) at any point in its production. Other alcoholic drinks, such as rum, gin, whisky or vodka, are not an issue.

The Biblical texts do not explain or justify the laws of kashrut. Some modern-day authors and lecturers have tried to analyse the ancestral rules and prohibitions in the light of science and modern times.

Philosophers may think that, by not mixing meat and dairy, Jews are refusing on moral grounds to mix milk, a symbol of life, with meat, a symbol of death.

Dieticians and nutritionists know from statistics that, because they have intermarried, Jews (especially Ashkenazim) often have higher than average cholesterol levels and that the rule separating milk and meat can reduce or stop triglyceride levels rising. Also, as there are no kashrut restrictions on vegetables, Israel is one of the countries with the highest number of vegetarians.

Another explanation comes from the fact that, in Judaism, all life is important if not sacred, including the life of animals. In this,

Judaism is not unlike Buddhism – or rather the other way round, in terms of chronology.

Kashrut is a priority but the preservation of life is a more important commandment. Thus, the rules can be overlooked in times of famine. Rabbis in the Warsaw ghetto allowed pork to be eaten because the lack of food was putting human lives at risk.

Hygiene is often given as the explanation for the origins of kosher customs. In hot countries at a time when hygiene was a luxury, it was advisable to stick to strict rules to avoid the spread of disease. Some Christian communities (the founders of Christianity were Jews who observed kashrut) thus followed kosher principles for centuries in the Middle East.

The halal dietary laws of Islam, a religion from the same part of the world and which also recognises Moses and Abraham, require the animal to be drained of its blood and prohibit pork, and therefore observe some of the Jewish kosher laws. Incidentally, Jews are not allowed to eat halal, but Muslims may eat kosher.

On the other hand, in other parts of the world like Asia, among Chinese populations in rural areas where hygiene is not always a priority, pork regularly forms the basis of the local diet.

Kashrut: a matter of religious rites, ancestral tradition, philosophical ethics or rules of diet and hygiene? Perhaps it is all of these.

PART II

SYLVIE JOUFFA'S RECIPES

*with the calorie content and nutrition tips
by Annick Champetier de Ribes*

STARTERS

Each recipe includes nutrition tips and recommendations for accompanying courses to create a balanced meal providing 500 calories per person.

Symbols

🏃 = how many people it serves

≡ = preparation time

⊟ = cooking time

🍷 = number of calories per person

STUFFED AVOCADOS
Israel

👥 Serves 4　　≡ 11 mins　　⧉ 11 mins

🍷 100 calories per serving

2 avocados
2 tomatoes
2 shallots

1 garlic clove
A few drops Tabasco sauce
Salt

Cut the avocados in half and discard the stones. Scoop out the flesh with a teaspoon leaving the skin intact.

Wash then dry the tomatoes and chop them into pieces.

Peel the shallots and garlic. Squeeze the lemon.

Blend all the ingredients and add a few drops of Tabasco according to taste.

Fill the avocado halves with this stuffing and serve as a starter.

Recommended accompaniments
Cochin cod, chachouka and exotic fruit salad.

Nutrition tips
Avocados have a high fat content (11%). They are naturally juicy so there is no need to add oily dressings.

EGGPLANT CAVIAR
Romania

👥 Serves 5　　≡ 15 mins　　⧉ 10 mins

🍷 45 calories per serving

1¼ lb eggplants
1 teaspoon crushed garlic

1 tablespoon sunflower oil
Salt, pepper

Cut the eggplants in half lengthwise.

Lay them on a baking tray.

Grill them for 5 minutes per side until the skins are lightly charrred.

Allow to cool and scoop out the flesh. Discard the skins.

Tip the flesh into the mixer. Add the oil and garlic. Season with salt and pepper and blend.

Arrange the eggplant caviar in a serving dish and chill for 1 hour in the fridge before serving.

Recommended accompaniments
Romanian roast kid, apple Kugel.

Nutrition tips
You can serve this eggplant caviar with 10g matzo (25 kcal).

From the nutritional point of view, eggplants are rich in magnesium and potassium. They are also a good source of fiber and can therefore help improve digestive transit.

COLESLAW
USA

Serves 6   15 mins

65 calories per serving

3 carrots	½ lemon
1 small Savoy cabbage	1 teaspoon sugar
4 tablespoons low-fat mayonnaise	Salt, pepper

Wash, drain and grate the cabbage.

Put the cabbage in a sieve and sprinkle with fine salt. Set aside for 15 minutes to draw out any bitterness. Then, rinse and drain.

Peel and grate the carrots. Squeeze the lemon half.

Put the grated carrots and cabbage into a bowl. Add the lemon juice, sugar, low-fat mayonnaise and a pinch of pepper. Season with salt to taste (NB: the cabbage has already been salted). Mix well and chill in the fridge for 1 hour before serving.

Recommended accompaniments
Beef pancakes, apple compote with raisins.

Nutrition tip
It is a good idea to blanch the cabbage for 5 minutes in boiling water to make it easier to digest. Cabbage is rich in calcium (430mg per 100g) and phosphorus. It is also an excellent source of vitamin C (200mg per 100g). Carrots are rich in carotene and vitamin A (12 000 IU per 100g).
This starter is ideal as part of a weight-loss diet.

CUCUMBERS IN CREAM
Poland, Russia

🧑‍🧒 Serves 6   🕐 5 mins

🍷 50 calories per serving

2 cucumbers
7 tablespoons 4% fat crème fraîche
½ bunch chives

1 cup fat-free yogurt
1 teaspoon lemon juice
Salt, pepper

Wash, drain and finely chop the chives. Peel the cucumbers. Cut them into quarters lengthwise and scoop out the central part containing the pips.
Cut them into thin strips about ½ cm thick.
Put them into a bowl. Season with salt and pepper and add the lemon juice, chives, yogurt and crème fraîche.
Mix well and chill everything in the fridge for at least 1 hour before serving.
These cucumbers in cream are excellent served with smoked salmon.
For variation, you can substitute dill or fresh mint for chives.

Recommended accompaniments
Spinach patties, 2 raisin cookies.

Nutrition tips
A low-calorie starter that provides plenty of calcium, protein and fiber.

In this recipe, the central part containing the pips is removed to make the cucumber easier to digest.

SPINACH WITH CHICKPEAS
Middle East

🧑‍🤝‍🧑 Serves 6   ≡ Prepare the day before, then 10 mins

🍳 1 hour   🍷 160 calories per serving

6½ cups spinach	2 teaspoons crushed sage
3 tablespoons olive oil	1 pinch bicarbonate of soda
1 lemon	Salt, pepper
1½ cups dried chickpeas	

The day before, put the chickpeas into a large bowl. Cover them with cold water and a pinch of bicarbonate of soda, and leave to soak over night.

Next day, rinse and drain the chickpeas. Then peel them by rolling them in your hands. Discard the skins. Bring a pan of salted water to the boil and simmer the chickpeas over a low heat for 1 hour.

Wash and drain the spinach. Squeeze the lemon and set the juice aside.

In a pan, bring 8 cups salted water to the boil. Add the spinach, cover with a lid and cook on a gentle heat for 15 minutes. Drain the spinach, squeezing out the water.

Arrange the spinach in a salad bowl. Add the chickpeas, olive oil, lemon juice and sage. Season with salt and pepper and stir everything thoroughly.

Recommended accompaniments
Moussaka, exotic fruit salad.

Nutrition tips
A starter that is high in fiber and protein (11g per serving).

The combination of spinach and chickpeas creates a dish that is especially rich in minerals, providing phosphorus, calcium and iron.

Sage is a plant that is grown for its medicinal and aromatic properties. It can make rich dishes easier to digest.

Low in fat and high in fiber with the additional benefits of the oil selected, this dish is recommended to help lower cholesterol.

CREAM CHEESE WITH PAPRIKA
Hungary

Serves 4   5 mins

100g per serving

2 cups 20% cream cheese
3 pickled gherkins
1 tablespoon paprika

½ lemon
Salt, pepper

Squeeze the lemon half and set the juice aside. Finely dice the gherkins.

Put the cream cheese into a salad bowl. Add the gherkins, paprika and 1 teaspoon lemon juice. Season with salt and pepper and stir everything thoroughly.

Place in the fridge and serve chilled as a starter.

This appetizer can also be made with fresh goats cheese.

Recommended accompaniments
Mixed platter of herring, coleslaw, eggplant caviar and 1 slice of cumin bread.

Nutrition tips
This makes a high-protein starter (10g per serving). You can serve it with an egg- or fish-based dish to top up your protein intake.

CHOPPED HERRINGS WITH APPLES
Poland

Serves 4   15 mins

150 calories per serving

4 fatty herring fillets
2 medium-sized onions

1 tablespoon sunflower oil
2 Golden Delicious apples

Peel the onions and slice them into fine rings. Peel the apples and chop them up into large chunks.

Blend the herrings, onions and apples and add the oil to obtain a thick cream. You can add a little oil if you think the mixture is too thick.

Chill the herring with apple pâté in the fridge and serve it as a starter with slices of toast or rye bread.

Recommended accompaniments
Potato cakes, creamy cheesecake.

Nutrition tips
1 slice of rye bread = 24 calories to add to this recipe.

This starter provides about 10g of protein per person.

It can be served with a salad and one or two dairy products for a low-fat dinner.

Herring is rich in Omega 3 fatty acids which can help combat heart disease.

The apples and onions also make this a high-fiber dish.

Two reasons to include it in a low cholesterol diet!

EGG AND MUSHROOM PÂTÉ
USA

🏃 Serves 4   ≡ 30 mins   ⏱ 10 mins
🍷 100 calories per serving

1 medium-sized onion	4 eggs
1 teaspoon sunflower oil	Salt, peppercorns
1¾ cups mushrooms	

Peel and slice the onion finely. Wash the mushrooms, then peel and cut them into thin slices. In an oiled, non-stick frying pan, sauté the onions until they turn transparent. Add the mushrooms and fry them gently, stirring until the juice has evaporated.

In a pan, bring 4 cups of salted water to the boil. Immerse the eggs for 10 minutes to harden. Then, drain and remove the shells.

In a bowl, mix together the hard-boiled eggs with the mushrooms and onions. Add a grind of pepper and a pinch of salt. Blend all the ingredients and arrange the mixture in a bowl. Chill for half an hour in the fridge before serving.

Serve this pâté with matzo or slices of cumin bread.

Recommended accompaniments
Veal with paprika, summer fruit salad.

Nutrition tip
A protein-rich starter (7g per person) that can also be used to increase your protein intake at dinner. Mushrooms are nutritionally valuable, being rich in protein (2.7%), potassium (450mg per 100g), phosphorus (130mg per 100g), iron (1 to 2mg per 100g), selenium (30mg per 100g) and in B group vitamins.

Add 25 to 50 calories per 10 to 20g matzo. A slice of cumin bread weighs 20g and provides 50 calories.

CHOPPED LIVER WITH CHIVES
Poland

Serves 4   15 mins   10 mins
190 calories per serving

1¼ lb chicken livers   2 hard-boiled eggs
1 bunch chives   1 large onion
1 tablespoon sunflower oil   Salt, pepper

Peel the onion. Blanch it for 3 minutes in a pan of boiling water. Drain and chop it up into large chunks.

In a pan, bring 4 cups salted water to the boil and simmer the chicken livers over a low heat for 10 minutes with the lid half on. Drain the chicken livers.

Shell the hard-boiled eggs.

Tip the chicken livers into a blender. Add the onion, oil, eggs and half the chives. Season with salt and pepper and blend.

Put the chopped liver in a serving dish and sprinkle with the rest of the chives. Chill in the fridge for 1 hour before serving with gherkins to garnish.

Recommended accompaniments
Raw vegetable salad, apple strudel.

Nutrition tips
This pâté is so high in protein (23g per serving) that it can constitute the main dish.

It is particularly rich in iron, a mineral it is often difficult to eat in sufficient quantity.

CHOPPED LIVER WITH PISTACHIOS
Greece

👪 Serves 6   ≣ 15 mins   ⬛ 10 mins
🍷 200 calories per serving

1¼ lb chicken liver	1 large onion
2 hard-boiled eggs	2 tablespoons olive oil
1 tablespoon shelled pistachios	Salt, pepper

Peel the onion. Roughly crush the pistachios with a pestle and mortar.

In a pan, bring 4 cups water to the boil and immerse the chicken livers. Cook them over a gentle heat for 10 minutes with the lid half on. Three minutes before the end of the cooking time, add the onion. Then, drain everything. Chop up the onion.

Peel the hard-boiled eggs.

Tip the chicken livers, onion, hard-boiled eggs and olive oil into the blender. Season with salt and pepper and blend.

Arrange the mixture on a serving dish. Add the pistachios and stir everything thoroughly.

Chill in the fridge for 1 hour before serving.

Recommended accompaniments
One matzo (10g = 25 calories), dressed lettuce, honey cake.

Nutrition tips
The same as for the chopped liver with chives.

Pistachios are rich in iron (7mg per 100g), potassium (970mg per 100g) and phosphorus (560mg per 100g).

They are high-energy nuts (630 kcal per 100g) due to their high fat content (54%).

CALVES' FOOT JELLY IN ASPIC
Poland, Russia

👥 Serves 6   ≡ Prepare the day before, then 30 mins.

🕒 3 hours   🍷 150 calories per serving

3 calves' feet, cut into three
½ bunch parsley
1 teaspoon dried thyme

3 garlic cloves
2 carrots
1 teaspoon crushed bay leaves
Salt, pepper

The day before, peel and crush the garlic. Peel the carrots and slice into rounds.

Put the calves' feet into a large pan with the carrots, garlic, thyme and bay. Season with salt and pepper and cover with 12 cups cold water. Put the lid on and leave to simmer over a gentle heat for 3 hours.

Wash, drain and chop the parsley. Then, drain the calves' trotters and set aside the broth.

Remove the bones from the calves' feet and discard. Blend the meat with the carrot.

Tip the mixture into a square earthenware dish. Add the broth and chopped parsley.

When the calves' feet are cold, put them in the fridge over night for the aspic to form.

Next day, cut the calves' foot jelly in aspic into large cubes with approximately 2 inch sides.

Serve seasoned with horseradish or vinegar.

Recommended accompaniments
This dish can be served as a *zakouski* (hors d'oeuvre) with a raw vegetables and eggs salad, chopped liver or herring, in which case you should halve the servings. You can add 20g matzo and serve fruit salad to finish.

Nutrition tips

This starter is an excellent source of protein (9g per serving).

It is not recommended if you are trying to reduce your cholesterol.

Thyme is high in thymol and therefore has significant antiseptic properties. It can also aid digestion.

Bay has antispasmodic properties and soothes heartburn.

SWEET PEPPER SALAD
Morocco

Serves 6   10 mins

60 calories per serving

4 sweet peppers (red,
  yellow and green)
½ bunch flat parsley
3 teaspoons paprika
1 pinch Cayenne pepper

½ bunch cilantro
½ lemon
3 teaspoons cumin
3 tablespoons olive oil
Salt, pepper

Wash the peppers, remove the stalks and cut them in half lengthwise. Discard the seeds and put them on an oven rack, skin side up.

Broil them for about 5 minutes until the skin is lightly charred. Set aside to cool, then peel and dice the peppers.

Wash the cilantro and parsley, drain and chop them finely. Squeeze the lemon half.

Put the peppers into a salad bowl. Add the olive oil, lemon juice, cumin, paprika, cilantro, parsley, a pinch of Cayenne pepper and salt and pepper.

Stir the pepper salad then place it in the fridge for half an hour before serving.

Recommended accompaniments

Moroccan chicken tagine, tea and date cake.

Nutrition tips

Peppers have a very high vitamin C content (120mg per 200g).

In order not to lose this benefit, avoid soaking the peppers when you wash them.

PURÉE OF EGGPLANTS WITH TOMATOES
India

🏃 Serves 4 ≡ 15 mins ⌛ 30 mins
🍷 60 calories per serving

3 eggplants
2 tomatoes
Juice of half a lemon
1 pinch Cayenne pepper
2 teaspoons ground
  cilantro
2 teaspoons turmeric
2 teaspoons ground masala

1 large onion
2 cloves of garlic
2 teaspoons grated fresh ginger
2 tablespoons olive oil
2 teaspoons ground cumin
½ bunch fresh cilantro
Salt

Peel the onion and slice it thinly. Peel and crush the garlic. Soak the tomatoes for 3 minutes in a pan of boiling water. Drain, peel and finely dice them. Wash, drain and trim the eggplants. Finely dice them. Squeeze the lemon half.

In an oiled frying pan, sauté the onion, garlic and ginger. Sprinkle with Cayenne pepper according to taste. Add the ground cilantro, cumin, turmeric and masala. Add the tomatoes and egg-plants. Season with salt and stir using a wooden spoon. Add 4 tablespoons water. Cover with a lid and cook gently for about 30 minutes, adding a little water as necessary.

Wash, drain and finely chop the fresh cilantro.

Arrange the purée of eggplants with tomatoes in a serving dish. Stir in the lemon juice, then scatter the fresh cilantro on top.

This purée of eggplants can be served with naan bread or slices of toast.

Recommended accompaniments
Fish with paprika, pistachio fondant.

Nutrition tips
If you eat this starter with naan bread, add 126 calories per serving.

This is a starter with plenty of flavor that will soon make you feel full.

Eggplants are fruit vegetables and always eaten cooked. They are a good source of potassium (220mg per 100g).

The garlic in this recipe boasts numerous benefits; in particular it can help lower blood pressure and cholesterol.

RADISHES WITH CREAM CHEESE
Poland

🏃 Serves 4   ⏲ 10 mins

🍷 75 calories per serving

1 cup 20% fat cream cheese	2 pickled gherkins
½ cup fat-free yogurt	½ lemon
1 bunch radishes	Salt, pepper

Trim the radishes then wash and drain them. Squeeze the lemon half.

Slice the radishes and gherkins into thin rounds.

Wash the chives and chop them up.

Put the radishes, gherkins, cream cheese, yogurt, chives and lemon juice into a salad bowl. Season everything with salt and pepper and stir.

Set aside in the fridge for 1 hour before serving.

Recommended accompaniments
Carp and hake fish cakes, four-fruit salad.

Nutrition tips
Low in fat and calories but high in protein (5g per person), calcium and fiber, this is a starter to indulge in!

TUNA ROLL
Italy

🏃 Serves 8   ≡ 10 mins   ⏲ 30 mins

🍷 150 calories per serving

2 × 5 ounce cans tuna in oil	5 tablespoons matzo meal
2 eggs	Salt
1¼ cups grated Parmesan	

Beat the eggs in a bowl.

In a salad bowl, place the tuna together with the oil, matzo meal and eggs. Season with salt, stir well and blend the ingredients.

Lay a piece of cling film on a large plate. Turn the mixture on to it, and using the cling film, roll it into the shape of a fat sausage. Then remove the cling film.

In a pan, bring 8 cups water to the boil with a big-mesh colander over it. Place the roll in the colander, put the lid on and steam gently for 30 minutes.

Next, carefully remove the roll and lay it on a serving dish. If it breaks, use a sheet of aluminium foil to press it back into shape. Leave to cool. Chill for 1 hour in the fridge and cut it into slices just before serving.

Recommended accompaniments
Raw vegetable salad, creamy cheesecake.

Nutrition tips
This is a protein-rich recipe (15mg per person) and should be treated as a main course.

Tuna is an excellent source of vitamins A and D and phosphorus.

It is also rich in Omega 3 fatty acids and is therefore particularly recommended to help combat heart disease.

This dish has a naturally high salt content, so it is not recommended for a low-salt diet.

CABBAGE AND APPLE SALAD
Hungary

🏃 Serves 6   ⏱ 15 minutes
🍷 100 calories per serving

3 eating apples	⅓ cup raisins
1 small-medium white cabbage	1 cup fat-free yogurt
½ lemon	1 teaspoon paprika
1 teaspoon strong mustard	Salt, pepper

Wash then dry the cabbage. Discard the stalk, and slice the cabbage into thin strips. Peel and core the apples. Cut them into quarters then into thin slices. Squeeze the lemon half.

In a salad bowl, mix together the yogurts, mustard, raisins, 2 tablespoons lemon juice, paprika and a pinch of salt and pepper. Add the cabbage and apples and stir everything together.

Recommended accompaniments
Carp with paprika, poppyseed biscuits.

Nutrition tips
A low-calorie recipe that has the added virtue of being high in fiber and calcium (200mg per person).

If you blanch the cabbage first for a couple of minutes, it will be easier to digest.

RAW VEGETABLE SALAD
Israel

👪 Serves 6   ≡ 20 mins   ⧉ 30 mins
🍸 80 calories per serving

4 medium tomatoes	1 fennel bulb
1 red bell pepper	1 celery heart
1 cucumber	1 dozen small white onions
2 medium-sized potatoes	½ bunch chives
½ bunch parsley	3 tablespoons olive oil
1 lemon	Salt, pepper
1 green bell pepper	

Put the potatoes in a pan. Cover them with salted water and cook for 30 minutes over a low heat with the lid on. Drain and peel. Peel the cucumber. Squeeze the lemon. Wash the parsley and chives. Drain them and chop them up finely. Wash then drain the tomatoes, peppers, fennel and celery. Remove the seeds from the peppers and tomatoes. Cut the cucumber into quarters lengthwise and scoop out the part with the seeds. Peel the onions and cut them in half. Finely dice all the vegetables.

In a salad bowl, mix together the olive oil and lemon juice, parsley and chives. Season with salt and pepper and add the vegetables.

Stir everything thoroughly and serve as a salad.

Recommended accompaniments
If you take out the potatoes, this starter can be served with any dish as part of a weight-loss diet.

Nutrition tips
The potatoes are not essential.

This recipe is particularly rich in fiber, potassium and vitamin C.

It is a good dish for appetite control and can help combat constipation, heart disease and cancer of the colon.

RAW VEGETABLES AND EGG SALAD
France

Serves 6   10 mins   10 mins
80 calories per serving

4 tomatoes	1 bunch chives
1 cucumber	3 tablespoons sunflower oil
1 Batavia lettuce	2 teaspoons red wine vinegar
2 eggs	Salt, pepper

Pour the oil and vinegar into a bowl. Season with salt and pepper and stir.

Wash and drain the chives, then chop them up finely.

In a pan, bring 2 cups salted water to the boil. Immerse the eggs in it and boil them for 10 minutes. Leave to cool then remove the shells. Cut them in half lengthwise. Scoop out the yolks and dice the whites. Crush the yolks in a garlic crusher.

Wash and dry the tomatoes and remove the stems. Cut them into rounds.

Peel the cucumber and cut them lengthwise into quarters. Scoop out the central part containing the seeds. Next, cut the cucumber into fine slices.

Separate the lettuce leaves then wash and drain. Cut a dozen leaves into strips. Set the rest aside for another occasion. Arrange the lettuce strips on a large serving dish. Then pile the slices of tomato, cucumber and hard-boiled egg white on top. Scatter the crushed egg yolks over everything. Pour the vinaigrette uniformly over the salad. Sprinkle with chives.

Recommended accompaniments
Beef with beans, orange cake.

Nutrition tips
This is a must in a weight-loss diet. Not only is it high in fiber, vitamins and potassium, but it is also low in calories.

The naturally high levels of carotene (pro-vitamin A) in tomatoes promotes good eye health.

FENNEL SALAD
Morocco

Serves 6   10 mins

80 calories per serving

4 fennel bulbs	3 tablespoons olive oil
½ lemon	½ bunch cilantro
½ bunch flat parsley	3 teaspoons paprika
2 teaspoons garlic granules	1 pinch Cayenne pepper
3 teaspoons cumin	Salt, pepper

Wash, drain and trim the fennel bulbs. Cut them lengthwise into thin slices.

Squeeze the lemon half. Wash, drain and finely chop the parsley and cilantro.

Put the fennel into a salad bowl. Add the oil, lemon juice, garlic, cumin, paprika, Cayenne pepper, parsley and cilantro.

Stir everything together and chill the fennel salad in the fridge for half an hour before serving.

Recommended accompaniments
Beef with lemon, exotic fruit salad.

Nutrition tips

This is a useful starter, not only because it is low in calories and high in fiber, but also because it is an excellent source of vitamin C (one serving of this salad provides all your daily requirements of vitamin C), vitamin A and iron.

The stalks and seeds of fennel are used in seasonings and the bulb as a vegetable.

Spices help regulate appetite control. In small quantities, they act as stimulants; in larger quantities, they make you feel full sooner.

MELON SALAD
France

Serves 4   5 minutes

70 calories per serving

1 large melon	½ lemon
1 medium slice water melon	4 mint leaves

Wash then drain the mint leaves. Squeeze the lemon half.

Cut the melon into quarters, remove the peel and scoop out the seeds. Then cut the flesh into cubes. Remove the peel from the water melon, scoop out the seeds and dice.

Mix the melon and water melon cubes in a shallow dish. Sprinkle with lemon juice.

Chill the melon salad in the fridge for 1 hour before serving in individual goblets, each with a mint leaf to decorate.

Recommended accompaniments

Italian beef with eggplants, apple meringue.

Nutrition tips

Melon is low in carbohydrates (5g per 100g). You can therefore eat it regularly without worrying about gaining weight.

One serving of this salad covers your recommended daily intake of vitamin A, which promotes good eye health.

Mint is a stimulant and aids digestion.

SMOKED SALMON WITH RED FRUIT
USA

Serves 4   10 minutes

220 calories per serving

14 ounce smoked salmon in thick slices
2 tablespoons balsamic vinegar
3 handfuls lambs lettuce
Peppercorns

2 cups mixed red fruit (strawberries, raspberries, redcurrants)
1 fennel bulb
1 lemon

Wash and drain the lambs lettuce. Wash and drain the fennel. Then cut it lengthwise into thin slices. Wash and drain the fruit. Cut the lemon into quarters.

Cut the salmon into 1¼ inch pieces. On each plate, arrange a bed of lettuce and slices of fennel. Add the smoked salmon and sprinkle the balsamic vinegar over it.

Season with a grind of pepper and add the red fruit. Lay a lemon quarter on the side of each plate.

Recommended accompaniments
Zucchini with eggs, baked apples with yogurt.

Nutrition tips
The high-protein content (24mg per person) of this recipe means you can treat it as a main course.

It is also rich in phosphorus and vitamins B6 and PP, which help maintain healthy bones.

Salmon is recommended to reduce the risk of heart disease thanks to its high levels of Omega 3 fatty acids.

TARAMOSALATA
Turkey

Serves 4   15 minutes
250 calories per serving

2 sacks smoked cod roe
1 lemon
½ baguette with the
   crust removed

4 tablespoons sparkling water
About 2 tablespoons
   sunflower oil

Soak the bread in cold water, then drain and squeeze dry.
Squeeze the lemon.
Using a sharp knife, cut open the cod roe sacks and remove the contents. Discard the skins.
Blend the cod roe with the bread and lemon juice, gently drizzling the oil into the mixture until the taramosalata has the consistency of thick mayonnaise.
Pour the mixture into a serving dish and stir in the sparkling water. This will thicken and blanch the mixture.
Chill the taramosalata for 1 hour in the fridge before serving. It can be served with blinis or matzos.

Recommended accompaniments
Chicken salad.

Nutrition tips
If you add matzos, (25 calories per cracker), this makes a high-calorie starter that provides a significant amount of protein (14g per person).
Fish eggs are very rich in sodium (880mg for 100g). The recipe is therefore not recommended as part of a salt-free diet.

SOUPS

BEET BORSCHT
Poland

Serves 6 ≡ 15 mins ⊞ 10 mins

60 calories per person

2½ cups cooked beets	3 eggs
2 tablespoons wine vinegar	Salt, pepper

Peel and grate the beets.

In a large pan, bring 8 cups salted water to the boil. Add the beets and cook over a gentle heat with the lid on for 10 minutes. Add 1 to 2 tablespoons wine vinegar to taste. Borscht should be slightly sour.

Strain the soup and discard the beets. You will obtain a clear, ruby-coloured broth. Break 3 eggs into a tureen, beat them lightly and pour over the hot soup a little at a time, stirring with a metal whisk. Blend the soup in the blender so that the eggs thicken the liquid.

Borscht is served cold with hot boiled potatoes if desired.

Recommended accompaniments
One potato, beef meatballs, apple and raisin compote.

Nutrition tips
The recipe is calculated without potatoes. If you include them, you should add 90 kcal per potato.

This broth is important in a weight-loss diet because it will stop you feeling hungry. It provides very few calories for a large quantity.

Beet is thought to be very sweet and is often prohibited in low-carbohydrate diets. In fact, it contains no more than 8g carbohydrate per 100 g. It would be a pity to exclude it; you only need to restrict the quantities per person.

RAPID RUSSIAN BORSCHT

👫 Serves 4   ⏲ 10 mins

🍷 50 calories per person

2 medium-sized, cooked
  beets
1 cup skimmed milk
½ lemon
1 cup mineral water

2 tablespoons 5% fat
  yogurt
1 teaspoon granulated
  sweetener

Peel the beets and chop them up. Squeeze the lemon half.

Blend the beets with the milk, crème fraîche, granulated sweetener and the lemon juice and water.

Pour the borscht into a tureen, then chill in the fridge for 1 hour before serving in 4 soup bowls.

This borscht can be served with boiled potatoes.

Recommended accompaniments
Zucchini with eggs, green salad with a dressing of one tablespoon rapeseed or olive oil, baked apples with yogurt.

Nutrition tips
You can eat as much of this soup as you like.

BORSCHT WITH SORREL
Russia

👫 Serves 6   ☰ 10 minutes   ⏲ 30 minutes

🍷 95 calories per serving

6½ cups sorrel
6 new potatoes
Yolk of 1 egg

1 lemon
Salt, pepper

Wash the sorrel, chop off the stalks, select some of the leaves and drain them.

In a pan, bring 6 cups salted water to the boil. Add the sorrel, cover with a lid and simmer over a low heat for 30 minutes.

Boil the potatoes in salted water for 30 minutes. Then drain them, set them aside to cool and peel.

In a tureen, beat the egg yolk. Add the soup a little at a time, stirring well. Season with salt and pepper.

Serve the borscht with sorrel with one potato per bowl.

Recommended accompaniments
Beef meatballs, salad of oranges with cinnamon and one raisin cookie.

Nutrition tips
Sorrel is very rich in vitamin C (124mg per 100g), carotene and phosphorus.

You should bear in mind, however, that it has a high oxalic acid content (300mg per 100g), so you should avoid it if you have suffered from oxalic lithiasis.

KRUPNIK
Poland

🏃 Serves 6   ≡ Prepare the day before, then 15 mins

🏃 1 hour 45 mins   🍷 180 calories per serving

9 ounce chicken giblets
3 cups dried cep
  mushrooms
1 large onion
3 carrots

1 cup fine pearl barley
1 cup navy beans
2 leeks
2 turnips
Salt, pepper

The day before, soak the navy beans and pearl barley in 4 cups cold water.

Next day, drain them. In a shallow bowl, cover the mushrooms with hot water and soak for 10 minutes. Then drain and finely dice them.

Peel and finely dice the carrots, leeks, onion and turnips.

In a large pan, bring 8 cups salted water to the boil. Add the pearl barley, navy beans and chicken giblets. Cover the pan with a lid and simmer gently for 1 hour.

Next, add the vegetables. Cover and simmer for a further 45 minutes.

Remove the giblets and use them in a separate dish or discard them.

Serve the soup piping hot.

Recommended accompaniments
Beef meatballs with onions or 100g meat stew and fresh fruit.

Nutrition tips
The chicken giblets are not included in the calorie content of this recipe.

This dish is a good source of slow sugars.

TOMATO SOUP
Hungary

Serves 6   10 mins   45 mins
100 calories per serving

10 medium tomatoes	1 tablespoon paprika
½ cup rice	Salt, pepper

In a pan, bring 4 cups water to the boil. Immerse the tomatoes in the water and heat for 3 minutes. Drain and peel. Next, blend them and set aside.

In a large pan, bring 12 cups salted water to the boil. Tip the rice in and simmer gently with the lid on. Then add the tomato purée and paprika. Season with salt and pepper, put the lid on and simmer for 15 minutes.

Serve the tomato soup hot.

Recommended accompaniments
Carp with paprika, winter fruit salad, one poppyseed cookie.

Nutrition tips
An excellent source of vitamin A.

GINGER SOUP
Morocco

Serves 6   15 mins   1 hour

200 calories per serving

1 lb 10 ounce chicken scallops	1 teaspoon dried dill tops
1 onion	1 tablespoon sugar
3 carrots	1 pinch ground nutmeg
2 shallots	1 clove
2 teaspoons ginger, fresh grated or ground	1 bay leaf
	Salt, pepper

Peel the onion and shallots and slice them thinly. Peel the carrots and cut them into rounds.

In a large pan, bring 8 cups salted water to the boil. Add the onion, carrots, garlic, shallots, ginger, dill, nutmeg, clove and bay leaf. Season with salt and pepper, put the lid on and simmer over a low heat for 30 minutes.

Next, add the chicken and sugar. Leave to cook over a low heat with the lid on for 30 minutes.

Serve the soup hot in individual bowls.

Recommended accompaniments
Orange cake, salad of oranges with cinnamon.

Nutrition tips
This recipe provides 25g protein per person and can be treated as a main dish.

Ginger makes it easier to digest fat.

PEARL BARLEY SOUP WITH MUSHROOMS
Poland

Serves 6   10 minutes   1 hour

160 calories per serving

1 cup fine pearl barley	2 cups dried cep mushrooms
6 carrots	Salt, pepper
2 turnips	

Soak the mushrooms in a bowl of warm water for 1 hour. Then drain them.

Peel the carrots and turnips.

In a large pan, bring 12 cups salted water to the boil. Add the pearl barley, carrots, turnips and mushrooms and season with salt and pepper. Cover with a lid and simmer for 1 hour. Remove the carrots, turnips and mushrooms using a slotted spoon. Blend them and put them back in the soup.

Adjust the salt and pepper to taste and serve the soup hot.

Recommended accompaniments
100g meat stew, apple kugel.

Nutrition tips
A recipe with plenty of potassium and good for intestinal problems.

FISH SOUP
India

Serves 4   **15 minutes**   **20 minutes**
260 calories per serving

14 ounce cod fillets cut into
  small chunks
9 ounce canned chickpeas
4 tomatoes
2 sweet bell peppers (red
  and green)
1 fennel bulb
4 shallots
2 garlic cloves

2 pinches Cayenne pepper
1 teaspoon turmeric
1 teaspoon cumin
1 litre fish poaching liquid
1 bunch flat parsley
1 bunch cilantro leaves
1 lemon
Salt, pepper

Drain the chickpeas. In a pan, bring 2 cups of water to the boil. Immerse the tomatoes in it for 3 minutes. Next, drain, peel and finely dice them.

Remove the stalks from the peppers and cut them in two lengthwise. Place them under the broiler for 5 minutes (or more), skin-side up, until the skins are charred. Peel them and cut them into thin strips.

Wash and trim the fennel bulb. Slice it finely from top to bottom.

Peel the shallots and slice them thinly. Peel and crush the garlic. Wash the parsley, mint and cilantro. Drain them, chop them finely and stir them together. Squeeze the lemon.

In a non-stick frying pan, sauté the shallots and garlic until the shallots turn transparent. Add the fennel slices and the pinch of Cayenne pepper. Sprinkle with the cumin and turmeric. Add the poaching liquid, tomatoes and peppers and bring to the boil. Add the fish, chick peas and half the herb mixture of parsley, mint and cilantro. Cover with a lid and cook over a low heat for 10 minutes.

Just before serving, sprinkle with the lemon juice and the remaining mixed herbs.

Recommended accompaniments
Pistachio fondant.

Nutrition tips
A main dish with a low-fat content.
Mint has stimulant and digestive properties.

CARROT VELOUTÉ
France

👪 Serves 8　　≣ 20 mins　　⌷ 50 mins
🍷 120 calories per serving

18–20 carrots	1 pinch dried crushed bay
1¼ lb potatoes	1 teaspoon ginger, fresh
1 pinch ground nutmeg	grated or ground
2 teaspoons olive oil	1 chicken bouillon cube
1 bunch chives	Salt, pepper
2 onions	

Peel the onions, carrots and potatoes. Slice the onions. Cut the carrots into fine rounds and dice the potatoes. Wash, drain and chop the chives finely.

In a non-stick frying pan, sauté the onions and carrots rapidly, stirring with a wooden spoon for about 2 minutes.

Pour 6 cups water into a large pan, add the bouillon cube, nutmeg, bay and ginger. Bring to the boil and add the carrots and onions. Season with salt and pepper. Cover with a lid and simmer gently for 45 minutes. Then, blend the soup.

Pour this carrot velouté into individual bowls. Sprinkle with the chives and serve hot.

Recommended accompaniments
Breaded scallops, raw vegetables and egg salad, one piece of fruit.

Nutrition tips
A good starter from the point of view of the calorie content and one that can improve digestive transit.

FISH DISHES

CARP AND HAKE FISH CAKES
Poland

Serves 8
40 mins
Prepare the day before, then 30 mins
250 calories / 27g protein per serving

1¼ lb carp fillets + bones
1¼ lb hake fillet + bones
2 eggs
3 large onions

2 carrots
1 tablespoon matzo meal
4 teaspoons sugar
Salt, pepper

The day before, peel the onions and carrots. Cut the carrots into rounds and set aside.

In a large pan, put 6 cups water, the fish bones and onion cut into rounds. Season with salt and pepper and add 2 teaspoons sugar. Put the lid on the pan and leave to simmer while you prepare the fish. Cut the 2 remaining onions into small chunks.

Blend the fish fillets with the onions, eggs, 2 teaspoons sugar and the matzo meal. Season with salt and pepper.

Moisten your hands and roll the mixture between them to form the fish cakes.

Put the fish cakes and slices of carrot into the poaching liquid. Half cover with the lid and simmer for about 35 minutes until the carrots are cooked. The fish cakes will be ready at the same time.

Using a slotted spoon, remove the fish cakes and arrange them on a serving dish.

Strain the liquid and pour it into a shallow bowl. Discard the bones. Add the onions and carrots to the juices. Put the fish and poaching liquid to chill over night so that the aspic forms.

Next day, serve the fish cakes cold with some of the aspic over them, and horseradish to garnish.

Along with chicken in broth, this is the most popular dish among East European Jews. It is made for the Jewish high holidays, Rosh Hashanah, Yom Kippur and Pesach.

Recommended accompaniments
Dressed green salad, creamy cheesecake.

Nutrition tips
The combination of a non-fatty with a semi-fatty fish that is rich in Omega 3 acids gives this dish the ideal nutritional properties for a weight-loss, low-fat diet.

COCHIN COD
India

🏃 Serves 8   ≡ 10 mins   ⟁ 20 mins
🍷 175 calories / 20g protein per serving

1 lb 6 ounces cod fillets cut into chunks	3 cloves of garlic
	1 onion
4 tomatoes	1 tablespoon curry powder
1 teaspoon cumin	1 pinch Cayenne pepper
1 teaspoon sweet pepper	1 teaspoon sunflower oil
1 bunch cilantro	Salt, pepper

Peel and dice the tomatoes. Wash, drain and finely chop the cilantro.

Peel the garlic and onion. Crush the garlic and slice the onion thinly. Sauté them in an oiled, non-stick frying pan.

Next, add the fish, tomatoes, curry powder, cumin, sweet pepper, Cayenne pepper and the salt and pepper. Add ½ cup water. Cover with a lid and simmer for 15 minutes.

Arrange the fish on a serving dish. Pour the sauce over it and sprinkle with cilantro.

You can serve this fish curry with white rice.

Recommended accompaniments
Rice with lentils, exotic fruit salad.

Nutrition tips
If you add 1¼ cups cooked rice per person, you should add 180 calories, giving you 350 calories per person per dish. This is still a sensible recipe for a weight-loss diet: fresh cod is a non-fatty fish providing B group vitamins as well as iodine and phosphorus.

CARP WITH PAPRIKA
Hungary

🏃 Serves 6   ≡ 20 mins   ⧇ 1 hour 30 mins

🍶 200 calories / 20g protein per serving

1 carp weighing 3 lb 5 ounces, cut into slices, with the head and tail	2 onions 1 bell pepper 1 tablespoon paprika
1 pinch Cayenne pepper 1 small can tomato paste	Salt, pepper

Wash, dry and deseed the pepper. Cut it into fine strips. Peel the onions and slice them finely.

In a large pan, put the fish head and tail together with the onions and pepper. Add 4 cups cold water, salt and pepper and simmer over a low heat for 1 hour.

Next, remove the fish head and tail and discard them along with the bones. Blend the poaching liquid and vegetables and pour the mixture back into a pan. Add the carp slices, paprika, Cayenne pepper and tomato paste. Season with salt and pepper, cover with a lid and leave to simmer for 30 minutes over a low heat.

The carp with paprika can be chilled over night in the fridge and eaten cold next day. The sauce will solidify.

Recommended accompaniments
Carrots with raisins, one blini with yogurt.

Nutrition tips
Carp from a fish farm is less fatty than wild carp (2g fat as opposed to 9g). It is a good source of vitamin A (300 IU).

SAUERKRAUT WITH PIKE
Russia

🏃 Serves 6   ≡ 15 mins   ⊞ 3 hours

🍷 200 calories / 25g protein per serving

1 pike weighing 1¾ cut into slices	2 tablespoons goose fat
8½ cups raw sauerkraut	3 onions
	Salt, pepper

In a pan, bring 6 cups salted water to the boil. Immerse the slices of pike in the water, cover with a lid and poach over a low heat for 15 minutes.

Peel and slice the onions thinly. Preheat the oven to 300 °F (Gas Mark 2).

In a high-sided pan, sauté the onions in the goose fat and add the sauerkraut. Stir everything together, put the lid on and simmer for 2 hours, stirring from time to time and adding a little water to prevent sticking.

Next, place a layer of sauerkraut in an oven dish. Arrange slices of fish on it, season with salt and pepper and cover with a second layer of sauerkraut. Sprinkle with 1 tablespoon water. Bake for 1 hour.

Recommended accompaniments
Stuffed avocados, honey cake.

Nutrition tips
Pike is a non-fatty fish and sauerkraut is also low in fat if bought raw; this explains the low-calorie content of this recipe. You should avoid it, however, if you suffer from digestive problems.

HAKE WITH CARROTS
Poland

🏃 Serves 6   ≡ 10 mins   ⊞ 1 hour

🍷 180 calories / 25g protein per serving

1lb 10 ounce hake, cut into slices	1 teaspoons granulated sweetener
3 carrots	Salt, pepper
2 onions	

Peel the carrots and cut them into slices.
Peel the onions and slice them thinly.
Place the hake in a pan, add the carrots, onions and sweetener.
Season with salt and pepper, half cover with a lid and simmer for
1 hour.

Recommended accompaniments
Yogurt with paprika, kasha, salad of oranges with cinnamon.

Nutrition tips
Hake is a non-fatty fish and a good source of iodine and magnesium, while carrots are high in fiber and carotene. This recipe
is ideal as part of a balanced weight-loss diet.

FISH COUSCOUS
Tunisia

Fish Soup – Fishcakes – Couscous

FISH SOUP

 Serves 6   20 mins   45 mins
 110 calories / 16g protein per serving

1¼ lb mullet, cut into slices	1 onion
2 tomatoes	1 small can tomato paste
2 carrots	2 turnips
2 zucchini	1 teaspoon sunflower oil
1 small slice of pumpkin	Salt, pepper

Peel the carrots, turnips, onion and pumpkin. Scoop out the seeds
from the pumpkin. Peel the tomatoes. Cut the carrots into
rounds. Slice the onion thinly and sauté it in an oiled, non-stick
frying pan.
    Wash, dry and trim the courgettes but do not peel them. Dice
the zucchini, turnips, pumpkin and tomatoes.
    Put the carrots, onions, turnips, tomatoes and tomato paste
into the couscous pan. Season with salt and pepper and cover

with cold water. Put the lid on, bring to the boil and cook gently for 15 minutes.

Add the pumpkin and cook for 10 minutes. Then add the fish and leave to cook for a further 15 minutes.

FISHCAKES

Serves 6   ≡ 15 mins   15 mins

70 calories / 8g protein per serving

2 cod fillets	1 onion
1 egg	2 tablespoons matzo meal
1 teaspoon sweet pepper	1 tablespoon dried parsley
1 teaspoon sunflower oil	Salt, pepper

Peel the onion and slice it thinly. Blend the cod with the onion.

In a shallow dish, mix the minced cod with the egg, matzo meal, paprika and parsley. Season with salt and pepper and stir everything well.

Moisten your hands and roll the mixture into fish cakes the size of ping-pong balls.

Oil a non-stick frying pan and sauté the fish cakes rapidly.

Next, put them into a high-sided pan, cover with water and simmer for 10 minutes over a low heat.

Serve the fishcakes with the fish soup and couscous.

COUSCOUS

Serves 6   ≡ 10 mins   5 mins

200 calories per serving

1¾ cups medium couscous	1 teaspoon margarine
1 teaspoon sunflower oil	Salt

In a high-sided pan, bring 2 cups salted water to the boil.

Tip the couscous into a shallow bowl. Add the water and oil and stir them into the couscous. Cover with a lid and leave the couscous to swell up for 5 minutes.

Next, add the margarine and separate the grains with a fork. Serve with the fish soup and fish cakes.

Recommended accompaniments
Plain raw vegetables, salad of oranges with cinnamon

Nutrition tips for the fish soup, fishcakes and couscous
The amount of couscous has been purposely limited to make this dish suitable for a weight-loss diet.

MACKEREL WITH TOMATOES
Romania

🏃 Serves 6   ≡ 15 mins   ⌘ 45 mins
🍷 250 calories / 20g protein per serving

6 boned mackerel, with
    heads and tails removed
5 tomatoes
½ cup dry white wine
3 onions
3 cups new potatoes

1 teaspoon dried thyme
1 teaspoon dried, crushed
    bay leaves
1 teaspoon sunflower oil
Salt, pepper

Preheat the oven to 400 °F.
    Peel the onions and slice them thinly. Peel and dice the tomatoes. Peel the potatoes and cut them into rounds.
    Arrange the mackerel in an oven dish. Cover them with the onions, tomatoes and potatoes. Sprinkle with the white wine, a drizzle of oil and the thyme and bay.
    Season with salt and pepper and cook in the oven for 45 minutes.

Recommended accompaniments
Pepper salad, blinis with yogurt.

Nutrition tips
Like many fatty fish, mackerel is high in Omega 3 fatty acid (4,000 to 5,000mg per 100g), and is recommended to help prevent heart disease.

FISH WITH PAPRIKA
Hungary

Serves 4   15 mins   15 mins

150 calories / 30g protein per serving

1 lb 6 ounce cod fillets, cut into cubes	1 red bell pepper
2 teaspoons olive oil	2 teaspoons paprika
2 cloves of garlic	4 shallots
1 tablespoon 5% fat crème fraîche	½ cup fat-free yogurt
1 green bell pepper	1 tablespoon cornstarch
	½ bunch cilantro

Wash, drain and finely chop the cilantro. Peel the garlic and shallots. Wash and drain the pepper, remove the stalks and seeds and cut them into thin strips.

In a bowl, mix the yogurt, crème fraîche and cornstarch.

Oil a non-stick frying pan. Place the fish in it, season with salt and pepper and sprinkle with paprika. Sauté it for a few minutes then set aside in a dish.

In the same frying pan and the fish juices, sauté the shallots, garlic and peppers. Add the fish and the mixture of yogurt and cornstarch. Cover with water and cook over a low heat for 5 minutes with the lid on.

At the end of the cooking time, sprinkle with cilantro.

You can serve this fish with paprika with white rice.

Recommended accompaniments
Fennel salad, cabbage with apples and raisins, one poppyseed cookie.

Nutrition tips
330 calories per serving if you add 1¼ cups white rice. The colour of peppers depends on how ripe they are. Before they are fully ripe, they are green then they turn yellow, orange and finally red. Red peppers are the sweetest.

TROUT AND MUSHROOM RAVIOLI (PIROSHKI)
Russia

🚶 Serves 5   ≡ 30 mins   ⊞ 15 mins

🍷 240 calories / 7g protein per serving of 3 ravioli cushions

INGREDIENTS FOR 15 RAVIOLI PILLOWS

8 ounce prepared pasta
3 ounce trout fillet
½ onion
1 cup cep mushrooms
1 teaspoon sunflower oil
1 teaspoon minced dill

1 teaspoon minced chives
1 tablespoon 5% fat crème
   fraîche
1 egg yolk
Salt, pepper

Preheat the oven to 300 °F.

Peel the onions and chop them up. Wash the mushrooms and slice them thinly.

Cut the trout fillet into small cubes. Set aside an egg yolk in a bowl, add a teaspoon water and stir.

Oil a non-stick frying pan and sauté the onions until they turn transparent. Then add the fish, the mushrooms, dill, crème fraîche and chives. Season with salt and pepper, stir everything together, cover with a lid and simmer for 5 minutes. Add half a glass of water as necessary. Pour everything into a shallow dish.

Roll out the pasta and use a whisky glass to cut rounds from it. Place a spoonful of the fish filling in the centre of each disc. Fold the disc in two and press the edges together firmly to close up the ravioli pillow. Use a pastry brush to coat the top of each pillow with the egg yolk.

Place all the ravioli on an oven tray lined with grease-proof paper.

Bake in the oven for 15 minutes until the ravioli pillows turn golden-brown, turning them over halfway through the cooking time and brushing the other side with egg yolk.

Recommended accompaniments
Coleslaw, lemon mousse cake with poppy seeds.

Nutrition tips
Trout is a non-fatty, freshwater fish. It is a good source of phosphorus, potassium and magnesium. This dish should be preceded by a starter and followed by a protein-rich dessert.

SARDINES WITH TOMATOES
Turkey

🏃 Serves 6   ≡ 15 mins   ⚎ 30 mins

🍷 150 calories / 25g protein per serving

1lb 10 ounce sardines	10 tomatoes
1 bunch parsley	1 tablespoon sunflower oil
3 lemons	Salt, pepper

Ask your fishmonger to clean the sardines and remove the scales and heads. Wash and drain them.

Wash, drain and finely chop the parsley. Squeeze the lemons.

In a pan, boil 4 cups water, immerse the tomatoes and blanch them for 3 minutes. Then drain, peel and dice the tomatoes.

In an oiled frying pan, sauté the tomatoes. Add 1 cup water, season with salt and pepper and cover with a lid. Cook over a low heat for 10 minutes. Then add the lemon juice and chopped parsley. Simmer for another 5 minutes.

Add the sardines and cook them gently with the lid on for 10 minutes. Turn them over and continue cooking another 10 minutes. Check the sauce and, if necessary, add water during cooking.

These sardines with tomatoes can be served with white rice.

Recommended accompaniments
Cucumbers in cream, spinach patties, one raisin cookie.

Nutrition tips
Add 180 calories for 1¼ cups white rice.

Sardines, like mackerel, are rich in Omega 3 fatty acids and help reduce the risk of heart disease.

SMOKED SALMON WITH EGGS
United States

🏃 Serves 6   ≡ 10 minutes   ⊡ 10 minutes

🍸 190 calories / 16g protein per serving

7 ounce slices of smoked salmon	1 teaspoon dried dill tops
8 eggs	1 teaspoon sunflower oil
1 onion	Salt, pepper

Peel the onion and slice it thinly.

Beat the eggs lightly in a bowl. Season with salt and pepper.

Cut the salmon into pieces.

In a non-stick frying pan, sauté the onion. Add the pieces of salmon. Sprinkle with dill and sauté rapidly. Turn the heat down and add the eggs, stirring continually with a wooden spoon.

Serve this dish hot.

Recommended accompaniments
Cabbage and apple salad, cheesecake.

Nutrition tips
Contrary to popular belief, smoked salmon is suitable for a weight-loss diet. It contains 180 calories and 22g protein per 100 g. It is a good source of Omega 3 fatty acids, which reduce the risk of heart disease.

POACHED SALMON TRIANGLES
France

🍴 Serves 5   ≡ 30 mins   ⊒⊑ 15 mins

🍷 145 calories / 3g protein per serving
(4 triangles per person)

INGREDIENTS FOR 20 TRIANGLES

10 sheets phyllo pastry
3 ounce fillet salmon
½ onion
75g boletus or Paris
   mushrooms
Salt, pepper

1 teaspoon sunflower oil
1 teaspoon minced dill
1 teaspoon minced chives
1 tablespoon 5% fat crème
   fraîche

Preheat the oven to 300 °F.

Peel and chop the onions. Wash and drain the mushrooms, then slice them thinly.

Cut the salmon fillet into small cubes. Oil a non-stick frying pan and sauté the onions lightly until they turn transparent. Add the fish, mushrooms, dill, crème fraîche and chives. Season with salt and pepper, stir, cover with a lid and simmer for 5 minutes. Add half a glass of water as necessary. Then, pour everything into a shallow bowl.

Separate the sheets of phyllo pastry one at a time. Cut them in half, then fold the half sheet in two. Place a teaspoon of filling at the top of the strip of phyllo pastry. Fold the corner over the stuffing. Fold the triangle over on itself several times as indicated on the phyllo pastry packet.

Arrange the triangles on an oven tray lined with grease-proof paper. Cook until golden-brown, turning them over half way through the cooking process.

Recommended accompaniments
Coleslaw, cheesecake.

Nutrition tips
This recipe is very low in fat (less than 2g per person) but also low in protein (3g per person). It should therefore be served with a protein-rich starter and dessert.

MEAT DISHES

PESACH LAMB (MSOKI)
Tunisia

👥 Serves 8   ≡ 30 mins   ⌛ 2 hours

🍷 450 calories / 30g protein per serving

3lb 5 ounce shoulder of lamb, cut into 8 pieces
13 cups spinach
3 carrots
3 zucchini
3 turnips
1 stick of celery
1 fennel bulb
4 cups scallions
3 cloves of garlic

⅔ cup fava beans
1 handful dried rose buds
½ bunch dill
½ bunch mint
½ bunch Italian parsley
½ bunch cilantro
1 tablespoon sweet paprika
2 flat round matzos
Salt, pepper

Wash and drain the vegetables, then dice them roughly with sides about ¾ inch.

Trim the spinach, then wash and drain it. Peel and crush the garlic. Wash the parsley, dill, mint and cilantro. Drain and chop them finely. Set aside the beans.

In a pan, bring 8 cups water to the boil. Put the beans to blanch for 3 minutes, then drain them and leave to cool. Remove the skins from the beans by rolling them in your hands and discard.

Put the meat and vegetables, herbs, garlic, celery, sweet paprika and crumbled rose buds in a high-sided pan. Season with salt and pepper and cover with water. Put the lid on and simmer gently, stirring from time to time, for 1 hour 15 minutes. Add the beans and cook for a further 30 minutes. Crumble the matzos and add them to the rest of the ingredients. If necessary, pour in a little water so that the cookies swell up. Cook for a further 15 minutes.

This dish is served at Pesach.

Recommended accompaniment
Summer fruit salad.

Nutrition tips
The natural fats in lamb (11g per 100g) give it an advantage in terms of flavor, so you do not need to add the cooking fats. This recipe is still suitable for a weight-loss diet.

ITALIAN BEEF WITH EGGPLANTS

👥 Serves 6   ≡ 20 mins   ⌛ 20 mins

🍷 220 calories / 38g protein per serving

INGREDIENTS FOR THE 1st STUFFING
2¼ lb ground beef   1 tablespoon paprika
2 cloves of garlic   1 pinch Cayenne pepper
1 onion   1 teaspoon olive oil
1 tablespoon ground cumin   Salt, pepper

INGREDIENTS FOR THE 2nd STUFFING
6 eggplants   9 ounce can chopped tomatoes
1 onion   Salt, pepper
2 cloves of garlic

For the 1st stuffing:
Peel and chop the onion and crush the garlic.
   In a large bowl, mix the ground beef with the garlic and onion. Season with salt and pepper, add the cumin, paprika, 1 pinch Cayenne pepper and stir everything together.
   Oil a non-stick frying pan and sauté the meat for 5 minutes. Preheat the oven to 400 °F.

For the 2nd stuffing:
Peel the onion and garlic.
   Cut the eggplants in half lengthwise. Lay the halves under the broiler and broil for 5 minutes, cut side up.
   Next, scoop out the flesh and discard the skins. Blend the eggplants with the onion, garlic and a pinch of salt and pepper.

In an oven dish, arrange a layer of the meat stuffing and cover with the eggplant stuffing.
Bake in the oven for 10 minutes and serve hot.

Recommended accompaniments
Melon salad, orange flower sponge cake.

Nutrition tips
You should choose 5% fat ground beef.
   Garlic is an aromatic plant and it is the bulb which is eaten. It can help prevent heart disease.

BEEF WITH LEMON
Tunisia

🏃 Serves 6   ≡ 15 mins   ⌷ 1 hour 40 mins
🍸 200 calories / 20g protein per serving

1lb 6 ounce shin of beef, cut into slices	1 tablespoon turmeric
	1 teaspoon sunflower oil
½ lemon	Salt, pepper
3 onions	

Squeeze the lemon half. Peel and thinly slice the onions. Sauté them in a non-stick frying pan.
   Add the beef and sauté it rapidly. Put everything into a high-sided pan. Season with salt and pepper, add the turmeric, lemon juice and enough water to cover. Put the lid on and simmer for 1 hour 30 minutes.
   You can serve this beef and lemon with white rice.

Recommended accompaniments
One serving of rice, fennel salad, summer fruit salad.

Nutrition tips
Add 180 calories for 1¼ cups white rice.
   This dish can be served with mushroom fricassee sautéed in a non-stick frying pan, which will only add another 40 calories.
   If the lemon has been treated with biphenyl, it should be

mentioned on the label. You should then wash it carefully in warm water.

Lemon juice has a very high vitamin C content (70mg per 100g). It is also used for preserving the colour of fruit and vegetables.

BEEF WITH SPINACH (TAFINA)
Algeria

👥 Serves 8   ≡ 15 mins   ⧮ 3 hours

🍶   340 calories / 26g protein per serving

2¼ lb breast of beef	3 cups new potatoes
13 cups spinach	7 ounce can chick peas
2 cloves of garlic	Salt, pepper

Peel the garlic cloves. Drain the chick peas. Trim the spinach, wash and drain it. Peel the new potatoes.

Place the spinach in a non-stick frying pan and wilt the leaves over a low heat, stirring with a wooden spoon.

Place the meat in a high-sided pan, add the whole garlic cloves, ½ cup water, salt and pepper, cover with a lid and cook gently for 1 hour.

Next, add the spinach and chick peas. Put the lid on and simmer for a further hour.

Finally add the potatoes and cook for another hour.

Recommended accompaniment
Winter fruit salad.

Nutrition tips
You can treat this as a main dish. It is rich in minerals, fiber and protein.

To keep the menu low in calories, serve fruit salad for dessert.

BEEF WITH BEANS
Tunisia

🍴 Serves 6   ≡ Prepare the day before, then 5 mins
⏲ 2 hours 30 mins 🍷 400 calories / 40g protein per serving

2¼ lb shoulder of beef   1 cup dried navy beans
3 cloves of garlic   2 teaspoons ground cumin
14 ounce can peeled tomatoes   1 70g tube harissa
1 bunch cilantro

The day before, soak the beans in cold water over night.
　　Next day, drain them. Peel and crush the garlic.
　　Wash, drain and finely chop the cilantro.
　　In a high-sided pan, put the meat, garlic, tomatoes and cumin. Season with salt and pepper and cover everything with cold water. Put the lid on and simmer gently for 1 hour 30 minutes.
　　Add the beans, put the lid back on and simmer gently for a further hour.
　　Fifteen minutes before the end of the cooking time, add the finely chopped cilantro.
　　Serve the beef and beans with harissa.

Recommended accompaniments
Raw vegetables and egg salad, orange cake.

Nutrition tips
Because of the fat in shoulder of beef (8g per 100g), this recipe does not need cooking fat.
　　Navy beans provide vegetable protein, slow-release carbohydrates and fiber. They are an excellent complement for the animal protein and iron supplied by the beef. This recipe constitutes a balanced main dish.

BEEF MEATBALLS
Poland

👪 Serves 6   ≡ 15 mins   🍲 15 mins

🍷 280 calories / 32g protein per serving

1lb 10 ounce lean ground beef	1 teaspoon garlic granules
2 eggs	1 tablespoon sunflower oil
2 tablespoons matzo meal	Salt, pepper

In a shallow bowl, mix together the meat, eggs, garlic, matzo meal, salt and pepper. Blend all these ingredients, adding ½ cup water.

Pour the mixture into a large bowl. Moisten your hands and form flat, oval meatballs.

Oil a non-stick frying pan and sauté the meatballs until they turn golden brown and are cooked inside.

Serve with horseradish.

Recommended accompaniments
Kasha, baked potatoes.

Nutrition tips
Provided you choose 5% fat ground beef, this makes a low-fat dish (8.5g per person) that is ideal as part of a weight-loss diet.

KEFTA MEATBALLS
Morocco

👪 Serves 6 (makes 30 meatballs) ≡ 30 mins 🍲 20 mins

🍷 180 calories / 18g protein per serving (per 5 meatballs)

INGREDIENTS FOR THE MEATBALLS

9 ounce ground beef	1 tablespoon sweet pepper
9 ounce ground veal	1 pinch Cayenne pepper
1 large onion	1 teaspoon cinnamon
2 cloves of garlic	1 teaspoon ginger, grated
1 tablespoon finely chopped parsley	or ground
	1 teaspoon ground cumin
1 tablespoon finely chopped cilantro	Salt, pepper

INGREDIENTS FOR THE TOMATO SAUCE

9 ounce can tomatoes,
chopped and peeled
½ bunch minced cilantro
1 teaspoon cinnamon

1 tablespoon paprika
1 pinch Cayenne pepper
Salt, pepper

Peel and crush the garlic.

In a shallow bowl, put all the meat, the garlic, onion, parsley, cilantro, paprika, 1 pinch Cayenne pepper, cinnamon, cumin and ginger. Season with salt and pepper and stir everything together. Then blend the mixture. Moisten your hands and form meatballs the size of walnuts.

In a high-sided pan, tip the chopped tomatoes and 2 large glasses of water. Add the sweet pepper, cinnamon, the Cayenne pepper and the cilantro washed, drained and chopped. Cover with a lid and simmer this mixture for 10 minutes. Season with salt and pepper.

Lastly, add the kefta meatballs and cook them uncovered over a low heat for 10 minutes.

Recommended accompaniments
Chachouka, compote of dried fruit.

Nutrition tips
A recipe packed with flavor and ideal for a weight-loss diet. The spices have antiseptic properties and are also antioxidants (which combat ageing, heart disease and cancer), and as they are highly flavored, you can cook this dish with a minimum of fat and salt.

VEAL MEATBALLS WITH ONIONS
Poland

Serves 6   20 mins   1 hour
260 calories / 23g protein per serving

1lb 6 ounces ground veal
1 large onion
2 eggs
1 clove of garlic
2 tablespoons matzo meal

1 tablespoon minced parsley
1 tablespoon sunflower oil
¼ lb can mushrooms
Salt, pepper

Peel and crush the garlic. Wash and drain the parsley, then chop it up. Peel and thinly slice the onion. Drain the mushrooms.

In a shallow bowl, mix together the meat, eggs, garlic, matzo meal and parsley. Season with salt and pepper and add ½ cup cold water. Blend this mixture.

Moisten your hands and form oval meatballs.

Oil a non-stick frying pan and sauté the meatballs for 1 minute on each side. Then place them in a high-sided pan.

In the same frying pan, sauté the onions until they turn transparent and add the meatballs and mushrooms. Cover with cold water. Season with salt and pepper, put the lid on and leave to simmer gently for 1 hour.

Serve the meatballs with horseradish.

Recommended accompaniments
Sweet pepper salad, apple kugel.

Nutrition tips
Veal needs to be cooked for a long time because it is rich in connective tissue. It contains varying amounts of fat according to the piece you buy (2% in a breast, 15% in a chop). Note that its high uric acid content (115mg per 100g) means that it is not recommended in cases of acute attacks of gout.

STUFFED MUSHROOMS
Turkey

🕺 Serves 4 ≡ 15 times ⚙ 25 minutes
🍷 140 calories / 14g protein per serving

12 large mushrooms	2 cloves of garlic
9 ounce skinless chicken breast	2 teaspoons dried parsley
1 onion	1 tablespoon matzo meal
2 tablespoons plain tomato sauce	1 teaspoon sunflower oil
	Salt, pepper

Wash the mushrooms, drain them, scrape them and remove the stalks.

Peel and crush the garlic. Peel the onion and slice it thinly.

Preheat the oven to 350 °F.

Blend the chicken, garlic, parsley and mushroom stalks.

Oil a non-stick frying pan and sauté this mixture for 5 minutes, seasoning with salt and pepper.

In a shallow bowl, mix together the meat with the tomato sauce and matzo meal. Arrange the mushroom caps (underside up) in an oven dish. Place a teaspoonful of stuffing on each one. If there is any left over, use it to make meatballs and put them to cook beside the mushrooms.

Bake in the oven for 20 minutes. Serve hot.

Recommended accompaniments
Raw vegetables and egg salad, lemon mousse cake with poppy seeds.

Nutrition tips
Mushrooms are richer than any other vegetable in vitamins and minerals (phosphorus, potassium, sulphur, iron and B group vitamins).

They also provide protein (2.7%) and their low calorie content gives them a special place in a weight-loss diet.

ROMANIAN ROAST KID

Serves 4   30 mins   1 hour

220 calories / 28g protein per serving

½ young goat	2 tomatoes
2 medium potatoes	1 green bell pepper
3 zucchini	1 teaspoon sunflower oil
2 onions	Salt, pepper
3 carrots	

If it is difficult to obtain goat from your butcher then shoulder of lamb can also be used.

Preheat the oven to 400 °F.

Peel the potatoes, carrots and onions. Peel the tomatoes and remove the stalk and seeds from the pepper. Wash, dry and trim the zucchini but do not peel them.

Finely dice all the vegetables. Then put them in an oven dish and cover them with water. Place the goat cut lengthwise on top and season with salt and pepper. Drizzle a little oil over the meat and roast in the oven for 1 hour.

Turn and baste the goat half way though the cooking time.

Recommended accompaniments
Eggplant caviar, 10g matzo, apple strudel.

Nutrition tips
Taking the potatoes out of this recipe only reduces it by 50 calories.
Goat is a lean meat (4% fat) and packed with protein (30%).

CHICKEN CHILI WITH BEANS
USA

👥 Serves 6   ≡ 15 mins   ⌇ 1 hour 15 mins
🍷 245 calories / 27g protein per serving

1lb 6 ounce skinless chicken breast	1 green bell pepper
	2 onions
1 14 ounce can tomatoes, peeled and chopped	2 cloves of garlic
	1 teaspoon ground cumin
1 14 ounce can kidney beans, cooked	1 pinch Cayenne pepper
	1 teaspoon sunflower oil
1 red bell pepper	Salt, pepper

Remove the stalk and seeds from the bell peppers. Cut them into thin strips.

Mince the chicken in the food processor. Peel the onions and garlic. Crush the garlic and finely slice the onions.

In an oiled, non-stick frying pan, sauté the meat rapidly, then turn it into a large pan. In the frying pan you have just used, sauté the onions. Tip the onions, garlic, chopped tomatoes, peppers, cumin, ½ cup water and Cayenne pepper into the pan. Season with salt and pepper, cover with a lid and cook over a low heat for 1 hour.

Lastly, add the beans, and simmer with the lid on for a further 15 minutes.

Recommended accompaniments.
Plain raw vegetables, one brownie.

Nutrition tips
A recipe full of vegetable and animal protein. Not recommended if you have intestinal problems.

STUFFED CABBAGE
Romania

Serves 6   30 mins   1 hour 30 mins

230 calories / 22g protein per serving

1 green cabbage	½ baguette, with the crust
11 ounce ground beef	removed
11 ounce ground veal	1 teaspoon sugar
2 cloves of garlic	Salt, pepper
1 onion	

INGREDIENTS FOR THE TOMATO SAUCE

5 tomatoes	1 pinch dried thyme
2 onions	1 pinch dried crushed bay
2 cloves of garlic	½ lemon
1 teaspoon sunflower oil	Salt, pepper
1 teaspoon sugar	

Soak the bread in cold water. Drain and squeeze out the water. Peel the onion and garlic; chop up the onion and crush the garlic. Wash the cabbage and remove the leaves.

In a large pan, bring 12 cups water to the boil. Put the cabbage leaves to blanch for 3 minutes. Drain them and set aside to cool.

In a large bowl, mix all the meat with the garlic, onion and bread. Season with salt and pepper. Form small meatballs from this mixture and place them in the centre of the cabbage leaves. Fold the sides in and roll up as though for Chinese spring rolls.

For the tomato sauce:
Bring 4 cups water to the boil and immerse the tomatoes for 3 minutes.

Next, peel and finely dice the tomatoes.

Peel the onions and garlic; chop up the onions and crush the garlic. Then sauté them in an oiled, non-stick frying pan.

Add the tomatoes, thyme and bay. Season the mixture with salt and pepper.

Squeeze the lemon half.

Cut the remaining cabbage into thin strips. Oil a high-sided pan and sauté the strips, sprinkling them with a teaspoon of sugar.

Add the stuffed cabbage leaves and cover them with the tomato sauce. Add the lemon juice. Check the seasoning and adjust to taste with salt, pepper and sugar. Put the lid on and simmer gently for 1 hour 30 minutes.

Recommended accompaniments
Calves' foot jelly in aspic, pear and apple compote.

Nutrition tips
This constitutes a main dish that is packed with flavor and does not need cooking fat.

Tomatoes are often used in weight-loss diets especially because they mean you don't have to use fat in the sauce. Very low in calories (20 calories per tomato), they are rich in vitamin C and carotene.

BEEF PANCAKES (BLINTZES)
Poland

👪 Serves 6   ≡ 1 hour 30 mins   ⬒ 40 mins

🍷 300 calories / 25g protein per serving

INGREDIENTS FOR THE PANCAKE BATTER

1 cup water   1 teaspoon sunflower oil
3 eggs   Salt
2¼ cups white flour

INGREDIENTS FOR THE FILLING

1¼ lbs ground beef   1 teaspoon sunflower oil
6 onions   Salt, pepper
1 tablespoon paprika

In a shallow bowl, prepare the pancake batter by mixing together the flour, eggs, water, oil and a pinch of salt. Blend the mixture then turn it into a bowl, cover and leave to stand for 1 hour.

Peel and slice the onions thinly. Sauté them in a non-stick frying pan. Add the meat and sprinkle with the paprika, salt and pepper. Cook over a low heat stirring continually for 10 minutes until the meat takes a golden colour.

Drop ladlefuls of batter into a non-stick frying pan. Heat the batter on one side then turn it over. Keep making pancakes until you have used up all the batter.

Fill the centre of each pancake with the meat. Fold in the sides and roll up.

Recommended accompaniments
Dressed salad, one brownie.

Nutrition tips
You should choose 5% fat ground beef.
You can treat this as a main dish and serve it with a salad.

BREADED SCALLOPS
Central Europe

🐄 Serves 6   ≡ 10 mins   ⌷ 10 mins

🍷 260 calories / 23g protein per serving

6 very thin veal slices	2 tablespoons sunflower oil
¾ cup matzo meal	1 lemon
2 eggs	Salt, pepper

Beat the eggs in a shallow bowl. Tip the matzo meal into another shallow bowl. Heat the oil in a frying pan.

Cut the veal slices in half. Dip them in the eggs and then in the matzo meal. Season with salt and pepper. Sauté them in the frying pan over a low heat for 5 minutes until they are golden-brown.

Next, dry them on kitchen roll. Drizzle the lemon juice over the breaded veal and serve with horseradish.

Recommended accompaniment
Raw vegetable salad, spinach with mushrooms, orange cake.

Nutrition tips
Veal contains varying amounts of fat according to the piece you buy (2% in a slice, 15% in a chop). Note that its high uric acid content (115mg per 100g) means that it is not recommended in cases of acute attacks of gout.

MOUSSAKA
Turkey

Serves 6   15 mins   30 mins

240 calories / 23g protein per serving

1 lb 6 ounce ground beef	3 cloves of garlic
6 tomatoes	2 tablespoons sunflower oil
6 eggplants	Salt, pepper
2 onions	

In a pan, bring 4 cups water to the boil.

Immerse 4 tomatoes and cook for 3 minutes. Drain and peel them. Dice them finely.

Cut the 2 remaining tomatoes into rounds and set aside. Peel and thinly slice the onions. Peel and crush the garlic and add it to the tomato chunks.

Preheat the oven to 400 °F.

Peel the eggplants and cut them into fat rounds.

In an oiled, non-stick frying pan, sauté the meat for 5 minutes. Season with salt and pepper, stir and set aside.

Use this frying pan to sauté the onions. Add them to the meat. Still using the same pan, add a little oil and sauté the eggplants for 5 minutes.

In an oven dish, place a layer of eggplants, cover with a layer of meat and add a layer of tomatoes. Repeat the process with a layer of eggplants then of meat. Finish with a layer of attractively arranged tomato rounds.

Bake in the oven for 30 minutes.

Recommended accompaniments
Spinach with chickpeas, exotic fruit salad.

Nutrition tips
You should choose 5% fat ground beef.
    Eggplants are rich in magnesium and zinc. They are a diuretic thanks to their high potassium content (260mg per 100g). They are low in calories (18 kcal per 100g) but should not be dipped in oil because they have a high absorption capacity.

CHICKEN PASTILLA
Morocco

🏃 Serves 8   ≡ 30 mins   ⏲ 1 hour 30 mins

🍷 380 calories / 33g protein per serving

1 chicken weighing 2½ lb	1 teaspoon ginger, grated
6 sheets phyllo pastry	or ground
3 onions	1 tablespoon margarine
4 eggs + yolk of 1 egg	½ teaspoon cinnamon
1¼ cups blanched almonds	1 teaspoon confectioner's
1 pinch saffron threads	sugar
¼ cup sugar	1 bunch cilantro
Tablespoon granulated	1 bunch parsley
sweetener	

Sauté the blanched almonds in a non-stick frying pan and chop them up.

    Peel and thinly slice the onions. Wash, drain and finely chop the cilantro and parsley.

    In a high-sided pan, put the chicken with the onions, ginger and saffron. Add 2 cups water. Season with salt and pepper, cover with a lid and cook over a low heat for 1 hour. Turn the chicken half way through the cooking time.

    Remove the chicken from the pan and put it in a shallow bowl. Leave to cool, then remove the bones and skin and cut it into small pieces. Only keep the flesh.

    Add the parsley, cilantro, cinnamon, sugar and sweetener to

the pan and reduce the cooking juices over a low heat uncovered for 5 minutes.

During this time, lightly beat 4 eggs and add them to the pan. Stir continually and cook over a low heat for 5 minutes. Then leave to cool.

Preheat the oven to 350 °F.

Place 3 sheets of phyllo pastry so that they overlap in a non-stick flan dish. Lay the chicken pieces on them, spreading them out well. Spread the herb and egg mixture over the chicken. Scatter almonds over the top and cover with 3 sheets of phyllo pastry brushed with margarine. Fold the edges down and use a pastry brush to coat the top with egg.

Bake in the oven for 20 minutes.

Just before serving, turn the pastilla on to a serving dish and decorate the top with icing sugar and cinnamon.

Serve hot.

Recommended accompaniments
Selection of plain raw vegetables, salad of oranges with cinnamon.

Nutrition tips
This pastilla should be treated as a main course.

Although there is no added fat, this recipe is high in fat (19g per person) and you should be careful what you have for dessert.

SWEET AND SOUR BEEF STEW
Central Europe

Serves 6   30 mins   2 hours 40 mins

350 calories / 35g protein per serving

2¼ lb brisket of beef cut into cubes	2 onions
3 carrots	3 tomatoes
1 white cabbage	⅓ cup raisins
1 lemon	¼ cup sugar
	Salt, pepper

Peel and dice the onions and carrots. Squeeze the lemon.

In a pan, bring 4 cups water to the boil and immerse the tomatoes for 3 minutes. Then, drain and peel them, scoop out the seeds and dice them finely.

Wash, drain and finely grate the cabbage.

In a pan, bring 6 cups water to the boil, immerse the cabbage for 3 minutes then drain it.

In a large pan, bring 8 cups of salted water to the boil. Put the meat in, season with pepper, cover with a lid and simmer for 1 and a half hours.

Next, add the carrots, tomatoes and onions. Cover with a lid and simmer gently for 1 hour.

Remove the meat, dice it and set aside. Add the cabbage, raisins and sugar to the pan, put the lid on and continue cooking for a further 30 minutes.

Lastly, add the pieces of meat and the lemon juice. Adjust the seasoning with salt, pepper and sugar.

Reheat the meat and vegetables for 5 minutes, then serve.

Recommended accompaniment
Honey cake

Nutrition tips
This makes a main dish with a high protein and fiber content.

Cabbage became popular throughout the Mediterranean countries in the Ancient World. The Greeks served cabbage soup to newly-weds on their wedding morning, which gave rise to a legend that children are born in cabbages!

CHICKEN IN BROTH
Poland

Serves 6   30 mins   1 hour

200 calories / 18g protein per serving

1 boiling chicken with giblets	1 onion
6 leeks	1 stick of celery
3 turnips	Coarse salt
3 large carrots	Salt and pepper

Wash, drain and peel the carrots, onion, leeks and celery stick. Tie the leeks together with white thread.

Place the chicken in a large pan and cover it with 12 cups water. Sprinkle it with coarse salt and pepper. Add the carrots, celery stick, turnips and onion. Half cover with a lid and simmer gently with the water just boiling for 30 minutes. Then turn the chicken over and cook for a further 30 minutes.

In another pan, bring 6 cups of salted water to the boil. Add the leeks. Cover with a lid and simmer gently for 30 minutes.

Remove the chicken from the pan, leave to cool then cut it into small chunks and arrange them in a serving dish.

Remove the carrots and turnips and put them with the leeks in another dish.

Strain the broth and pour it into a tureen.

Serve the chicken on individual plates, with horseradish and gherkins.

Serve the broth separately in soup bowls with the vegetables.

If you like, you can add *knaidelach* (matzo balls) or *kreplech* (ravioli) to the broth.

Recommended accompaniments
Raw vegetables and egg salad, apple strudel.

Nutrition tips
Chicken accounts for 90% of the poultry on the market. It is always a young male.

It is a particularly lean meat (5g fat per 100g) if you avoid eating the skin. It has a mild flavor and can be cooked in a variety of ways.

SPICY COCHIN CHICKEN
India

👥 Serves 6   ≡ 10 mins   ⏲ 45 mins

🍷 160 calories / 22g protein per serving

1 and a half chickens, cut into 12 portions	4 shallots
3 cloves of garlic	2 teaspoons ginger, fresh grated or ground
1 bunch cilantro	1 teaspoon turmeric

Stuffed cabbage

Starters (chopped liver with chives, taramosalata, aubergine (eggplant) caviar, herrings)

Bortsch

Potato
cakes

Fromage frais (yogurt) and raisin ravioli

Matzo balls

Spices

Fromage frais (creamy) cheesecake

Stuffed carp

Pesach lamb

Stuffed tomatoes and peppers

Spinach with chick peas

Cochin cod

Rice with
lentils

Fennel
salad

Smoked salmon with red berries

Chachouka tart

Cabbage and apple salad

1 pinch Cayenne pepper	1 teaspoon sunflower oil
1 tablespoon curry powder	3 tomatoes
½ lemon	Salt, pepper

Wash, drain and finely chop the cilantro.

Peel the garlic and shallots. Wash and dry the tomatoes. Blend the garlic, shallots, ginger and tomatoes, then set aside. Squeeze the lemon half.

In an oiled frying pan, sauté the chicken. Then put it into a high-sided pan. Add the mixture you have just blended. Sprinkle with curry powder, turmeric and Cayenne pepper. Season with salt and pepper, cover with water, put the lid on and simmer gently for 45 minutes. The chicken must be tender and fall away from the bone (if necessary, increase the cooking time).

Add the juice of the lemon half and sprinkle with the cilantro just before serving.

Recommended accompaniments
Rice with lentils, exotic fruit salad.

Nutrition tips
This recipe is particularly low in calories. Accompanied with vegetables (mushrooms, carrots or spinach), it can be combined with a richer starter or dessert.

STUFFED CHICKEN
Poland

🚶 Serves 6   ≡ 30 mins   ⌱ 1 hour 15 mins
🍷 340 calories / 30g protein per serving

1 chicken weighing about	2 eggs
3 lb 5 ounce	1¼ lb chicken livers
2 tablespoons matzo meal	1 teaspoon sunflower oil
1 onion	Salt, pepper

If you ask in advance your butcher will bone the chicken and leave the skin on the chicken. Remove the flesh from the carcass and bones.

In a pan, bring 4 cups water to the boil. Put the chicken livers to simmer for 5 minutes. Drain them. Peel the onion and cut it into chunks.

In a shallow bowl, mix together the chicken livers, chicken flesh, eggs, matzo meal and the onion. Season with salt and pepper and blend everything. Preheat the oven to 400 °F.

Stuff the chicken with this mixture, restoring to it its original shape as far as possible. Then, sew up the apertures at either end with white thread.

Lay the chicken in an oiled oven dish. Roast in the oven for 1 hour 10 minutes. Turn it half way through the cooking time and baste it from time to time with water.

Serve slices of the stuffed chicken with horseradish.

Recommended accompaniment
Carrots with raisins, exotic fruit salad.

Nutrition tips
This is an iron-rich recipe that is also full of vitamin B12 and protein.

It is ideal to combat tiredness.

KREPLECH – CHICKEN RAVIOLI
Poland

🏃 Serves 3 (15 ravioli pillows)

≣ Leave to stand for 1 hour, then 30 mins   ⏲ 15 mins

🍷 390 calories / 24g protein per serving of 5 ravioli pillows

INGREGIENTS FOR THE PASTA DOUGH
1⅔ cups white flour   2 tablespoons cold water
1 egg white   1 pinch salt

INGREGIENTS FOR THE STUFFING
9 ounce chicken breast   1 teaspoon sunflower oil
1 onion   Salt, pepper
1 teaspoon dried parsley

In a shallow bowl, mix together the flour, egg white, water and salt. Put a cloth over the bowl and leave to stand for 1 hour.

Peel the onion and slice it thinly. Grind the chicken breast in a food processor.

In an oiled frying pan, sauté the minced chicken and set aside. Sauté the onion.

In a salad bowl, mix together the chicken, onion and parsley; season with salt and pepper.

Roll the pasta dough out thinly with a rolling pin. If it sticks, add a little flour. Cut 4 inch squares from the dough. Place a teaspoonful of the filling in the middle of each square. Fold the edges over from top to bottom and gather them together to form small pillows. Press the edges down to close firmly.

In a large pan, bring 8 cups of salted water to the boil.

Immerse the chicken ravioli pillows in it and simmer gently (the water should be just boiling) for 10 minutes.

Next, drain them with a slotted spoon taking care not to tear them.

Recommended accompaniment
Raw vegetable salad, one piece of fresh fruit.

Nutrition tips
This recipe is particularly low in fat (5g per person) and high in slow-release sugars and protein.

CHICKEN SALAD
Turkey

Serves 6   20 mins   1 hour

200 calories / 18g protein per serving

1 chicken	1 stick of celery
1 onion	2 scallion stalks
1 bunch parsley	2 tablespoons olive oil
1 lemon	Salt, pepper
2 carrots	

Squeeze the lemon. Wash and drain the parsley and chop it finely. Peel the carrots. Wash and drain the potatoes.

In a pan, bring 6 cups of salted water to the boil. Put the chicken in, cover with a lid and simmer with the water just boiling for 15 minutes.

Next, add the whole carrots and simmer for 15 minutes. Remove the chicken and drain the carrots. Leave everything to cool.

Remove the skin and bones from the chicken. Cut the flesh into small chunks. Discard the skin and bones.

Peel the onion and chop it up.

Cut the carrots, celery stick and scallion stalks into small chunks. In a salad bowl, mix the oil with the lemon juice and season with salt and pepper. Taste it and adjust the seasoning accordingly.

Add the chicken, carrots, celery, onion, scallion stalks and chopped parsley.

Stir everything thoroughly and chill for a few moments in the fridge before serving.

Recommended accompaniments
Taramosalata, melon salad for dessert.

Nutrition tips
Don't forget that parsley is an excellent source of vitamin C (200mg per 100g) and minerals (iron, calcium, sulphur and potassium).

This is a totally balanced dish and ideal as part of a weight-loss diet.

MEAT STRUDEL
Central Europe

🚶 Serves 6   ≡ 30 mins   ⌛ 20 mins
🍷   340 calories / 22g protein per serving

1 8 ounce sheet shortcrust pastry	1 tablespoon paprika
11 ounce ground veal	1 onion
11 ounce ground beef	2 teaspoons sunflower oil
	Salt, pepper

Preheat the oven to 400 °F. Peel the onions and slice them thinly.
Pour 1 teaspoon of oil into a non-stick frying pan. Sauté the

onions and meat. Sprinkle with paprika and season with salt and pepper.

Roll out the pastry and place a thin layer of meat over the whole surface area. Fold in the sides and roll up the pastry. Place this roll in an oven dish.

Drizzle a little oil over it and cook in the oven for 20 minutes.

Recommended accompaniment
Dressed green salad, pear and apple compote.

Nutrition tips
You should choose 5% fat ground beef.

MOROCCAN CHICKEN TAGINE

Serves 6   Marinate over night, then 30 mins
1 hour   200 calories / 23g protein per serving

1 and a half chickens, skin removed, cut into 12 portions	1 tablespoon cumin
	4 teaspoons ginger, grated or ground
4 onions	2 tablespoons sweet pepper
4 zucchini	1 teaspoon saffron powder
6 carrots	1 pinch saffron threads
1 9 ounce can tomatoes, peeled and chopped	4 cloves of garlic
	½ bunch parsley
1 lemon	½ bunch cilantro
2 preserved lemons	1 pinch Cayenne pepper
1 tablespoon olive oil	Salt, pepper

The day before, squeeze the lemon. Peel and crush the garlic.

Place the chicken pieces in a large shallow bowl. Add 1 table-spoon olive oil, the lemon juice, crushed garlic, 2 teaspoons grated ginger, 1 tablespoon sweet pepper and 1 teaspoon saffron powder. Stir everything together, cover with a plate and set aside in the fridge over night.

Next day, peel the onions and slice thinly. Wash and drain the zucchini, trim them and cut them lengthwise into three then into small sticks. Peel the carrots and cut them into small sticks. Wash and drain the cilantro and parsley and chop them up finely. Discard the pulp from the 2 preserved lemons and set aside the peel.

Drain the chicken pieces and set aside in the marinade.

Sauté the chicken in a dry non-stick frying pan, without oil. Put the meat in a high-sided pan. Add the marinade.

Sauté the onions in the frying pan you have already used, then add them to the pan with the chopped tomatoes and carrots. Season with salt and pepper and add 1 tablespoon sweet paprika, 1 pinch of Cayenne pepper, 1 teaspoon grated ginger and 1 pinch of thread saffron.

Add 1 large glass of water, season with salt and pepper, cover with a lid and simmer for 15 minutes.

Next, add the zucchini, preserved lemon peel and the chopped parsley and cilantro. Put the lid on and cook over a low heat for 45 minutes.

Recommended accompaniments
Fennel salad, tea and date cake.

Nutrition tips
The spices used have antiseptic and antioxidant properties (the latter help combat ageing, heart disease and cancer), and because they are full of flavor, you do not have to use so much fat or salt.

STUFFED TOMATOES AND PEPPERS
Turkey

Serves 10　　　15 mins　　　35 mins
200 calories / 22g protein per serving

5 large, firm tomatoes	3 slices of bread
3 green bell peppers	2 teaspoons ground sweet
2¼ lb ground beef	pepper
2 cloves of garlic	1 tablespoon sunflower oil
2 tablespoons dried	2 teaspoons sugar
parsley	Salt, pepper

Wash and dry the tomatoes and peppers. Cut the tops off, about a quarter of the way down. Scoop out the pulp from the lower part of the tomatoes and set aside. Discard the pepper seeds. Keep the upper parts of the vegetables, which will be used as 'lids' when they are stuffed. Peel and crush the garlic.

Soak the bread in cold water. Drain and squeeze out the water.

In a large bowl, prepare the stuffing. Mix the meat with the garlic, dried parsley, sweet pepper, the bread and 1 teaspoon of sugar. Season with salt and pepper and add 4 tablespoons water. Blend this mixture.

Oil a non-stick frying pan and sauté the meat for 5 to 10 minutes until it is cooked.

Next, stuff the vegetables with this filling. Cover them with the tops, which you set aside.

Place the stuffed peppers in a high-sided pan. Add the tomato pulp and two glasses of water. Season with salt and pepper, add 1 teaspoon of sugar, cover with a lid and simmer gently for 15 minutes.

Lastly, add the stuffed tomatoes and continue cooking for a further 10 minutes.

Recommended accompaniments
Eggplant caviar, 1 × 10g matzo, apple meringue.

Nutrition tips
You should choose 5% fat ground beef.

This is a highly coloured, highly flavored low-calorie recipe that you can indulge in as much as you like!

VEAL WITH PAPRIKA
Hungary

🧑‍🤝‍🧑 Serves 6   ≡ 15 mins   ⧉ 1 hour 20 mins

🍸 330 calories / 24g protein per serving

1 lb 6 ounce veal for , poaching with the bones removed, diced	1 tablespoon paprika
	1 teaspoon ground cumin
	1 teaspoon dried thyme
1 cup pearl barley	1 teaspoon dried bay
1 cup tomato sauce	1 teaspoon sunflower oil
3 cloves of garlic	1 tablespoon basil
1 onion	Salt, pepper

Bring 4 cups water to the boil. Immerse the pearl barley and simmer with the lid on for 30 minutes. Drain the pearl barley.

Peel the garlic and onion, chop the onion and crush the garlic. Wash and drain the basil, then chop it up finely.

In an oiled, non-stick frying pan, sauté the meat until it turns golden-brown.

Then turn the meat into a high-sided pan. Sauté the onions.

Add to the pan the garlic, onions, paprika, pearl barley, tomato sauce, thyme, bay and cumin. Stir everything together, add ½ cup water, salt and pepper, cover with a lid and cook gently for 1 hour 15 minutes.

Add the basil and leave to cook for a further 5 minutes.

Recommended accompaniments
Sweet pepper salad, orange cake.

Nutrition tips
Pearl barley is the kernels of barley grain. It is a good source of slow-release sugars.

Don't forget the garlic, which is known to have numerous advantages; in particular it helps lower high blood pressure and cholesterol.

VEAL CHOLENT
Central Europe

🧍 Serves 6   ≡ Prepare the day before, then 30 mins

⌛ 2 hours 15 mins   🍷 365 calories / 28g protein per serving

1 lb 6 ounce veal for
  poaching, without bones,
  cut into chunks
3 carrots
2 cloves of garlic
1 tablespoon paprika
1 bay leaf
1 teaspoon sunflower oil

1 large onion
¾ cup dried navy beans
½ cup pearl barley
2 potatoes
1 teaspoon cumin grains
2 tablespoons wine vinegar
Salt, pepper

The day before, soak the navy beans in a large bowl of cold water.

Next day, peel and thinly slice the onion. Peel and crush the garlic. Peel the potatoes and carrots. Drain the navy beans. Cut the carrots into rounds.

In a large pan, bring 4 cups water to the boil.

Oil a non-stick frying pan and sauté the veal, then put it in a large pan.

Sauté the onions and add them to the veal with the carrots, pearl barley, navy beans, cumin, paprika, vinegar and the bay. Season with salt and pepper and stir everything thoroughly. Place the potatoes on top of everything.

Cover with a lid and simmer for 2 hours.

Recommended accompaniment
Pear and apple compote, 1 cinnamon cookie.

Nutrition tips
This makes a balanced main course with a low fat content but plenty of animal and vegetable protein, vitamins, minerals and fiber.

It is a good recipe to help combat heart disease.

VEGETABLES AND SIDE DISHES

KNAIDELACH – MATZO BALLS WITH EGGS
Poland

Serves 20   **1 hour**   **15 mins**

170 calories per serving of 8 matzo balls

INGREDIENTS FOR 80 MAZTO BALLS

3 cups matzo meal	4 eggs
2 tablespoons sunflower oil	Scant I cup water
Salt, pepper	

Break the eggs into a large bowl, beat, then add the water. Season with plenty of salt and a little pepper. Sprinkle the matzo meal into the eggs, stirring thoroughly with a wooden spoon to obtain a thick dough.

Cover the dish and leave to stand for 1 hour. The mixture should form a thick dough. Add water or matzo meal as needed.

Then, moisten your hands and form little balls the size of walnuts. Arrange them on a large tray, spreading them out so that they do not touch.

In a large pan, bring 8 cups salted water to the boil and put the matzo balls to simmer, uncovered, for 15 minutes.

Using a slotted spoon, press any balls that bob up to the surface back down. Next, remove them carefully using the slotted spoon and arrange them on a serving dish.

Serve the matzo balls in the chicken broth. They can also be sautéed and served as an accompaniment to meat dishes.

Recommended accompaniments
Plain raw vegetables, chicken in broth, apple kugel.

Nutrition tips
It is sometimes a good idea to halve the quantities (which then gives you only 85 calories per serving of 4 matzo balls), and serve with green vegetables.

TSIMMES – CARROTS WITH RAISINS
Central Europe

🧑‍🤝‍🧑 Serves 6   ≡ 10 mins   ⏢ 35 mins

🍷 140 calories per serving

18–20 carrots	1 tablespoon honey
1 teaspoon ground cinnamon	1 tablespoon margarine
⅔ cup raisins	Salt, pepper

Peel the carrots and cut them into rounds.

Put the raisins to swell up in a bowl of hot water for 5 minutes. Then drain them.

In a pan, bring 4 cups salted water to the boil. Put the carrots in and simmer gently with the lid on for 30 minutes, then drain them.

Heat the margarine in a frying pan. Tip the carrots in, sprinkle with cinnamon, add the honey and raisins and season with salt and pepper. Stir and sauté gently for 2 minutes. Taste and adjust the seasoning with honey, cinnamon or salt.

Carrots with raisins are traditionally served at the Rosh Hashanah meal to make sure the coming year is sweet.

Recommended accompaniments
Stuffed chicken, summer fruit salad.

Nutrition tips
The nutritional benefits of carrots are many: they help prevent heart disease as well as certain cancers and the ageing of cells, and they help maintain good eye health and regulate digestive transit.

Contrary to popular belief, carrots contain only 7g carbohydrates per 100g and are ideally suited to a weight-loss diet.

STUFFED CABBAGE
Turkey

Serves 6   15 mins   40 mins
100 calories per serving

1 green cabbage	3 onions
½ cup long-grain rice	1 lemon
2 teaspoons sunflower oil	Salt, pepper

Peel and thinly slice the onions. Squeeze the lemon. Select the leaves from the cabbage and wash them.

In a pan, bring 4 cups water to the boil. Blanch the cabbage leaves for 3 minutes, then drain.

Preheat the oven to 400 °F.

In an oiled, non-stick frying pan, sauté the onions, then the rice. Add 3 ladles cold water. Season with salt and pepper, cover with a lid and simmer for 13 minutes. Next, place 1 tablespoon of this filling on each cabbage leaf. Fold in the sides of the leaf and roll up. If there are any leaves left over, cut them into strips.

Lay the stuffed cabbage leaves in an oven dish. Arrange the strips of cabbage around them. Add water to half way up. Sprinkle the lemon juice over them and add a drizzle of oil. Season with salt and pepper.

Bake in the oven for 30 minutes.

Recommended accompaniments
Eggplant caviar, 1 × 10g matzo, cheesecake.
Or chicken salad and one raisin cookie.

Nutrition tips
This dish gives you two thirds of a day's calcium requirements and all the daily vitamin C requirements.

CABBAGE WITH APPLES AND RAISINS
Poland

👫 Serves 6   ≡ 30 mins   ⊞ 1 hour 30 mins
🍸 120 calories per serving

1 green cabbage
1 tablespoon sugar
1 teaspoon cinnamon
2 Golden Delicious apples
⅔ cup raisins

1 lemon
1 onion
1 teaspoon sunflower oil
Salt, pepper

Put the raisins to swell up in a bowl of warm water.

Peel and core the apples, cut them into quarters then into slices.

Wash and drain the cabbage. Cut it into quarters, remove the stalk and cut it into thin strips.

In a large pan, bring 8 cups water to the boil. Blanch the cabbage for 3 minutes, then drain it. Peel and thinly slice the onion. Squeeze the lemon. Drain the raisins. Oil a large, high-sided pan and sauté the cabbage, onion and apples rapidly. Cover everything with water.

Add the sugar, cinnamon and raisins and season with salt and pepper. Put the lid on and leave to simmer for 1 hour 30 minutes, stirring occasionally.

At the end of the cooking time, the water should be absorbed. Serve this cabbage with raisins as a side dish with meat courses.

Recommended accompaniments
Melon salad, fish with paprika, 3 poppyseed cookies.

Nutrition tips
This side dish is packed with vitamins and minerals.

It is rich in calcium, magnesium, iron and vitamin C.

It is also ideal for a low-fat diet.

RUSSIAN PICKLED CUCUMBERS
Russia and Poland

🏃 Serves 6 ≣ 15 minutes, marinade for 8 days

🍷 40 calories per serving

2¼ lb cucumbers about 4-4½ cm long
1 bunch fennel (or dried fennel seed)
3 cloves of garlic

5 cups coarse salt
1 bunch parsley
1 bunch thyme and bay
20g peppercorns
Oak or vine leaves

Wash and rub dry the cucumbers. Peel the garlic but leave the cloves whole.

In a large ceramic or glass jar, place a layer of oak or vine leaves. Add a layer of cucumbers then a layer or herbs mixed with garlic cloves and peppercorns. Sprinkle generously with coarse salt. Repeat the operation until there are no more cucumbers left. Cover everything with cold boiled water or mineral water. On the top layer of cucumbers lay a piece of wood with weights on it (or stones).

Leave the cucumbers to stand for 8 days at room temperature. They are then ready to be eaten. Don't worry, if a white film forms on top of the cucumbers: it is not mold and can just be removed.

Russian pickled cucumbers are eaten at any occasion and served with meat and poultry.

Recommended accompaniments
Chopped liver and all meat dishes.

Nutrition tips
To be consumed without moderation, provided you are not on a low-sodium diet.

ZUCCHINI WITH EGGS
Central Europe

🚶 Serves 4   ≣ 10 mins   ⌷ 10 mins
🍷 130 calories per serving

4 zucchini   2 teaspoons sunflower oil
1 onion   Salt, pepper
4 eggs

Trim then peel the zucchini. Grate them using the coarse blade.
Peel and thinly slice the onions.

Break the eggs into a shallow bowl, season with salt and
pepper and lightly beat them.

In an oiled, non-stick frying pan, sauté the onions. Add the
zucchini and eggs.

Leave to cook over a low heat for 5 minutes, turning with a
wooden spoon.

Recommended accompaniments
Hake with carrots, yogurt and raisin ravioli.

Or yogurt with paprika, 1 × 10g matzo, compote of dried
fruit.

Nutrition tips
This dish contains 7g protein per person. It can be served either
as a vegetable side dish, or to top up your protein intake at
dinner.

COUSCOUS WITH MINT AND THYME
Algeria

🚶 Serves 8   ≣ Prepare the day before, then 30 mins
⌷ 2 hours   🍷 250 calories per serving

2¾ cups medium couscous   1 cup dried wild mint (*flio*)
1 tablespoon sunflower oil   and 1 cup dried wild thyme
Salt, pepper   (*zatar*), sold in Middle
                                    Eastern groceries

The day before: in a large pan, bring 6 cups water to the boil. Put a third of the mint and a third of the thyme in a shallow bowl. Add the boiling water, put the lid on and leave to infuse over night.

Next day, sieve the herbs, discard them and retain the infusion.

Tip the couscous into a large basin and pour 2 cups of infusion over it. Moisten the grains thoroughly and leave to stand for 30 minutes.

Put a third of the mint and a third of the thyme in the couscous pan. Three-quarters fill the couscous pan with cold water. Cover with a lid and bring to the boil.

Oil the couscous strainer using kitchen roll. Oil your hands and roll the couscous around in them. Tip the couscous into the strainer and poke a spoon handle through the grains here and there to create funnels through which the steam can escape.

Cook uncovered for 45 minutes. Pour the couscous back into the basin. Moisten it with 2 ladlefuls of infusion. Season with salt and pepper, stir in 1 tablespoon oil and leave to stand for 15 minutes.

Put the couscous back in the strainer, bring the water to the boil and cook for 20 minutes. Leave the lid off and aerate with the spoon handle again.

Turn the couscous back into the basin. Add a ladleful of the infusion and leave to stand for 5 minutes. Add the remaining herbs, stir them in then separate the grains again with your hands.

Serve this couscous with herbs with meat.

Recommended accompaniments
Kefta meatballs, salad of oranges with cinnamon.

Nutrition tips
This recipe is completely fat free.

Mint is a stimulant and aids digestion.

QUICK COUSCOUS
Morocco

🏃 Serves 6   ≡ 10 mins   ⊠ 5 mins

🍷 200 calories per person

1¾ cups medium couscous
1 teaspoon sunflower
  oil

1 teaspoon margarine
Salt

In a pan, bring 2 cups salted water to the boil.
    Tip the couscous into a shallow bowl. Add the water and oil.
Stir, cover with a lid and leave to swell up for 5 minutes.
    Next, add the margarine and separate the couscous grains with
a fork.
    Serve hot.

Recommended accompaniments
Moroccan chicken tagine, salad of oranges with cinnamon.

Nutrition tips
The amount of couscous has been purposely restricted to make
this suitable for a low-fat diet.

SPINACH WITH MUSHROOMS
Italy

🏃 Serves 6   ≡ 10 mins   ⊠ 15 mins

🍷 55 calories per serving

13 cups spinach
7 cups cep or white
  mushrooms
3 cloves of garlic

1 tablespoon fresh basil
1 teaspoon olive oil
Salt, pepper

Wash, drain and finely chop the basil. Trim the spinach, then
wash and drain it. Wash and scrape the mushrooms, then slice
them finely. Peel and crush the garlic.
    In an oiled, high-sided pan, sauté the mushrooms and garlic.
Next, add the spinach and season with salt and pepper. Cover

with a lid and leave to simmer for 8 minutes, stirring occasionally to prevent the vegetables sticking.

Recommended accompaniments
Melon salad, Italian beef with eggplants, tea and date cake.

Nutrition tips
This side dish accounts for almost all the daily vitamin and mineral requirements and provides no more than 55 calories per person.

SPINACH PATTIES
Turkey

🏃 Serves 6 ≡ 15 minutes ⌇ 20 minutes
🍷 190 calories per serving

6½ cups spinach
1 cup matzo meal
½ bunch cilantro
6 eggs

1½ cups fat-free yogurt (optional)
1 teaspoon sunflower oil
Salt, pepper

Separate the egg yolks from the whites. Put the egg whites in a shallow bowl with a pinch of salt. Whisk them until stiff. Wash, drain and finely chop the cilantro.

Wash and drain the spinach, then chop it finely by hand.

Put the spinach, egg yolks and matzo meal into a shallow bowl. Season with salt and pepper and stir thoroughly. Carefully fold in the stiff egg whites.

Oil a non-stick frying pan and use a wooden spoon to place heaps of the mixture in the pan to form small blini-style patties.

Serve these spinach patties hot sprinkled with cilantro.

If you are eating a meal without meat, you should add 1 teaspoon yogurt per patty.

Recommended accompaniments
Cucumbers in cream, sardines with tomatoes, one raisin cookie.

Nutrition tips
Spinach is rich in potassium and calcium. It also contains a large amount of iron (3mg per 100g), although very little of this is absorbed by the body.

This dish provides 9g protein per person. It can be served as a side dish with steamed fish, or you can put it with a salad to top up your protein intake.

LATKES – POTATO CAKES
Poland

👨‍👩‍👧 Serves 6   ≡ 20 mins   ⏲ 15 mins
🍷 200 calories per serving

4 large potatoes	Optional: 1 tablespoon
2 eggs	granulated sweetener
⅓ cup white flour	Salt, pepper

Beat the eggs in a bowl.

Peel the potatoes and grate them on the coarse blade. Place them in a strainer and press down on them to extract the liquid.

Put the potatoes into a shallow bowl with the flour and eggs. Season with salt and pepper and mix everything together.

Moisten your hands and form little balls, then flatten them; they should be the size of a child's hand. Press them again to squeeze out any liquid.

Put the potato cakes to cook in a non-stick frying pan, 5 minutes per side, until they turn golden brown.

Serve them sprinkled with sweetener as a dessert or else unsweetened as a side dish with meat.

Recommended accompaniments
Raw vegetables, veal meatballs with onions.

Nutrition tips
This dish provides 6g protein per person.

Potatoes are rich in potassium (500mg per 100g).

KASHA – BUCKWHEAT
Central Europe

Serves 6   **5 mins**   **15 mins**
130 calories per serving

1½ cups buckwheat
1 large onion
1 teaspoon sunflower oil

1 pinch paprika
Salt, pepper

Peel and thinly slice the onion.

Sauté the onion in an oiled, non-stick frying pan. Add the buckwheat. Stir and sprinkle with paprika, salt and pepper. Add 2 cups of water. Bring to the boil, cover with a lid and simmer gently for 10 minutes.

Check the cooking and stir occasionally with a wooden spoon. Add water as necessary.

At the end of the cooking time, the water should be absorbed and the grains should separate easily.

Serve the buckwheat with chicken or other meat dishes.

Recommended accompaniments
Beef meatballs, baked apples without yogurt.

Nutrition tips
Buckwheat is high in fiber.

You can reduce the quantities by adding carrots cut into rounds. In that case, you should prepare ½ cup buckwheat and 12 carrots; this recipe would provide 100 calories.

VEGETABLE KUGEL
Turkey

Serves 12   30 mins   1 hour

120 calories per serving

10 carrots	4 cups spinach
3 eggs	1 cauliflower
1 pinch ground nutmeg	6 teaspoons olive oil
1 clove of garlic	¾ cup matzo meal
1 teaspoon dried thyme	Salt, pepper

Preheat the oven to 400 °F.

Peel and crush the garlic. Peel the carrots and cut them into small rounds.

In a pan, bring 1 litre water to the boil. Heat the carrots for 10 minutes to soften them. Drain, then leave to cool and blend them with the thyme, ¼ cup matzo meal, 1 teaspoon olive oil, 1 egg and a pinch of salt and pepper. Set aside in a bowl. Wash the blender bowl.

Wash the cauliflower and break it up into florets. Bring 4 cups water to the boil and simmer the cauliflower for 7 minutes. Next, drain and blend it with ¼ cup matzo meal, 1 egg, 1 teaspoon olive oil and a pinch of salt and pepper. Set everything aside in another bowl and wash the blender.

Trim then wash and drain the spinach. In a large pan, bring 4 cups water to the boil and cook the spinach for 5 minutes. Drain it and blend with 1 egg, the garlic, nutmeg, ¼ cup matzo meal, 1 teaspoon olive oil and salt and pepper. Set aside in a bowl.

Oil a non-stick soufflé mould. Put a layer of cauliflower purée into it, a layer of spinach purée and finish with layer of carrot purée. Bake in the oven for 20 minutes.

You can bake this vegetable kugel in individual moulds, if you prefer. In that case, they will only need 15 minutes in the oven.

Recommended accompaniments
Romanian roast kid, honey cake.

Nutrition tips
This recipe is a feast for the eyes as well as tasty and nutritious.

HORSERADISH
Poland

🏃 Serves 6 ≡ 5 mins

🍷 20 to 40 calories per serving

1 medium jar white horseradish	2 tablespoons white wine vinegar
1 tablespoon sugar	

Pour the horseradish into a bowl.

Add 4 tablespoons water, the vinegar and the sugar. Stir everything together, taste and add sugar and water to sweeten the mixture, as necessary.

Transfer the mixture to a larger, airtight jar and store in the fridge.

Recommended accompaniments
Horseradish is served with most Jewish dishes in Eastern Europe, especially meat, fish cakes and stuffed carp.

Nutrition tips
You can eat as much horseradish as you like, unless you have digestive problems.

RICE WITH LENTILS
India

🏃 Serves 6 ≡ 15 mins ⚎ 30 mins

🍷 245 calories per serving

1¼ cups long-grain rice	1 clove of garlic
½ cup red lentils	⅓ cup raisins
1 onion	Salt, pepper

Peel the onion and garlic. Crush the garlic and thinly slice the onion.

Put the raisins to swell up in a bowl of hot water for 5 minutes, then drain them.

In a non-stick frying pan, sauté the onion and garlic until the onion turns transparent. Add the rice, lentils and raisins.

Stir and add 3 cups water. Season with salt and pepper. Cover with a lid and simmer for about 25 minutes until the water is absorbed. The cooking time depends on the quality of the lentils. Taste and add water or continue the cooking time accordingly.

Recommended accompaniments
Cochin cod, baked apples with yogurt.

Nutrition tips
This dish contains no fat and is therefore suitable for low-cholesterol diets.

To reduce the calories, you can halve the amounts and add a salad.

ONION SOUFFLÉ
France

🪶 Serves 6   ≡ 15 mins   ≡⊡≡ 30 mins
🍷 100 calories per serving

4 onions	¼ cup matzo flour
1 egg	1 tablespoon sunflower oil
6 egg whites	Salt, pepper

Preheat the oven to 325 °F. Peel and thinly slice the onions.

In an oiled, non-stick frying pan, sauté the onions until they turn transparent.

Mix the onions in a bowl with the whole egg, 1 egg white, the oil and the matzo flour. Season with salt and pepper.

Whisk the 5 egg whites to stiff peaks, adding a pinch of salt. Fold them carefully into the rest of the ingredients.

Pour everything into a non-stick soufflé mould and bake in the oven for 25 minutes until the top is golden brown.

Recommended accompaniments
Plain raw vegetables, hake with carrots, creamy cheesecake.

Nutrition tips

An unusual side dish and good from the nutritional point of view
as an accompaniment with meat or a mild-flavoured fish.

TABOULEH
Libya

🏃 Serves 10   ⏱ 15 mins

🍷 240 calories

2¾ cups medium couscous	1 bunch mint
2½ cups tomato juice	6 tablespoons olive oil
5 tomatoes	3 lemons
1 large onion	Salt, pepper
1 bunch flat parsley	

Peel the onion and dice it finely. Wash then drain the mint and
parsley. Finely chop the herbs.

In a large pan, bring 8 cups water to the boil and immerse the
tomatoes for 3 minutes. Drain, leave to cool, then peel them and
dice them finely. Squeeze the lemons.

In a large bowl, put the couscous together with the olive oil,
tomato juice, onion, mint and parsley. Season with salt and
pepper and stir everything thoroughly. Lay a plate on top and
place the tabouleh in the fridge for 2 hours before serving.

Recommended accompaniments

Tuna roll, salad of summer fruits.

Nutrition tips

A dish of slow-release sugars and therefore ideal for a low-cholesterol diet.

CHACHOUKA TART
Algeria

👥 Serves 6   ≡ 15 mins   🍳 40 mins

🍷 255 calories per serving

1 short-crust pastry base	3 red bell peppers
3 green bell peppers	10 tomatoes
3 cloves of garlic	1 tablespoon olive oil
3 teaspoons sweet pepper	1 pinch Cayenne pepper
1 pinch dried thyme	Salt, pepper
1 pinch crushed bay leaves	

Peel and crush the garlic.

In a large pan, bring 4 cups water to the boil. Heat the tomatoes for 3 minutes. Drain, peel and dice the tomatoes.

Wash and trim the peppers and cut them in half lengthwise. Deseed them and place them on an oven rack, skin-side up.

Broil for about 5 minutes until the skin chars. Leave them to cool, then peel and finely dice the peppers.

Preheat the oven to 400 °F.

Oil a non-stick frying pan and sauté the peppers with the tomatoes, garlic, sweet pepper, thyme, bay, Cayenne pepper and a pinch of salt and pepper.

Add 2 tablespoons water. Cover with a lid and cook gently for 10 minutes. Remove the lid and leave the juices to reduce for 10 minutes, turning the mixture from time to time with a wooden spoon.

Line a quiche case with the pastry, then pile the mixture into it and bake in the oven for 30 minutes.

Recommended accompaniments
Fennel salad, cheesecake.

Nutrition tips
Don't forget to serve protein with this dish.

CHACHOUKA
Morocco

Serves 8 20 mins 30 mins
55 calories per serving

10 tomatoes
3 cloves of garlic
1 pinch Cayenne pepper
1 tablespoon sweet pepper
1 bunch cilantro

6 red and green bell peppers
1 teaspoon olive oil
1 tablespoon cumin
1 bunch flat parsley
Salt, pepper

In a pan, bring 8 cups water to the boil and immerse the tomatoes for 3 minutes. Next, drain, peel and finely dice them. Peel and crush the garlic.

Wash and trim the peppers and cut them lengthwise in half. Deseed them and place them on an oven rack, skin-side up.

Broil for about 5 minutes until the skin chars. Leave them to cool, then peel and dice them. Wash then drain the cilantro and parsley and chop them up finely. Tip the tomatoes, peppers, garlic, cumin, sweet pepper, Cayenne pepper and parsley into a high-sided pan. Season with salt and pepper and add the olive oil and 1 tablespoon water. Cover with a lid and cook gently for 30 minutes, stirring from time to time.

At the end of the cooking time, add the cilantro. Serve hot or cold. Chachouka makes a good side dish for poultry.

Recommended accompaniments
Moroccan chicken tagine, orange cake, salad of oranges with cinnamon.

Nutrition tips
The ideal accompaniment for any meat, fish or egg dish.
You can eat as much of it as you like.

STUFFED TOMATOES
Algeria

 Serves 6   15 mins   30 mins

 140 calories per serving

6 large tomatoes
7 cups mushrooms
4 onions
6 anchovy fillets
2 cloves of garlic

2 egg yolks
2 tablespoons breadcrumbs
2 teaspoons sunflower oil
Salt, pepper

Preheat the oven to 400 °F.

Wash and dry the tomatoes. Slice the top off each one. Half remove the flesh from the lower part of the tomatoes. Peel and thinly slice the onions. Peel and crush the garlic. Peel, wash and drain the mushrooms and chop them up finely. Crush the anchovies.

In an oiled, non-stick frying pan, sauté the onions, mushrooms and garlic after seasoning with salt and pepper. Tip this mixture into a large bowl. Add the anchovies and egg yolks. Fill the tomatoes with this stuffing. Sprinkle with breadcrumbs and drizzle the oil over the top.

Arrange the stuffed tomatoes in an oven dish. Add a glass of water to the base of the dish and bake for 20 minutes.

Recommended accompaniments
Smoked salmon with eggs, blinis with yogurt.

Nutrition tips
Leave out the anchovies if you are on a salt-free diet.

TOMATOES WITH CHEESE AND EGGS
Turkey

 Serves 4   20 mins   10 mins

 200 calories per serving

4 tomatoes
1 tablespoon sunflower oil
2 cups sheep's cheese or feta

4 eggs
Salt, pepper

Bring 4 cups water to the boil in a large pan. Immerse the tomatoes and heat for 3 minutes. Drain and peel the tomatoes, cut them into quarters, remove the seeds and dice them finely.

In an oiled frying pan, sauté the tomatoes for a few minutes. Dice the cheese and add the chunks to the pan. Stir the cheese into the tomatoes and sauté.

Break the eggs over the pan, stir them in and season with salt and pepper. Cover with a lid and cook gently for 2 minutes. Serve hot.

Recommended accompaniments
Raw vegetable salad, yogurt and raisin ravioli.

Nutrition tips
You should use low-fat 25% fat cheese. This recipe provides 17g protein per person. Treat as a main dish and serve with salad.

DESSERTS

POPPYSEED COOKIES
Russia

🧍 Makes 30 cookies   ≡ 20 mins   ⏱ 23 mins
🍷 70 calories per cookie

3½ cups white flour
⅔ cup granulated sugar
1 tablespoon granulated
  sweetener
¼ cup poppy seeds
½ teaspoon baking powder
1 egg

½ teaspoon bicarbonate
  of soda
2 egg whites
2 tablespoons orange juice
3 teaspoons grated orange peel
1 teaspoon grated lemon peel

Preheat the oven to 350 °F.

Put the poppy seeds into a pan and cover with water. Heat for 3 minutes until they swell up, then drain.

In a shallow bowl, mix the flour, sugar, sweetener, poppy seeds, bicarbonate of soda and baking powder. Add the egg, egg whites, orange juice and orange and lemon zest.

Stir vigorously, divide the dough into two portions and form 2 loaves measuring approximately 10 inch by 1½ inch thick. Cut them into three and arrange on a baking tray lined with a sheet of greaseproof paper. Bake for 15 minutes.

Remove the cookies from the oven, allow to cool, then cut into diagonal slices about ¾ inch thick. Put them back in the oven for 5 minutes, then turn them over and bake for a further 5 minutes. They should be golden brown on top.

Store in a metal cookie tin.

Recommended accompaniments
Melon salad, fish with paprika, cabbage with apples and raisins.

Nutrition tips
You should always wash citrus fruit in warm water before grating.

From the calorific point of view, 1 piece of fruit can replace 1 biscuit.

RAISIN COOKIES
Morocco

👪 Makes 25 cookies   ⏲ 1 hour soaking, then 10 mins
⏲ 15 mins   🍷 64 calories per cookie

⅔ cup raisins
½ cup low-fat butter
  (42% fat)
⅓ cup confectioner's sugar
1 tablespoon sweetener

1 egg
½ cup ground almonds
¾ cup cornstarch
2 tablespoons orange
  flower water

Preheat the oven to 300 °F.

In a bowl, put the raisins to swell up in the orange flower water for 10 minutes. Meanwhile, put the butter to stand at room temperature so that it softens. Drain the raisins.

Then, in a shallow bowl, stir vigorously the egg, ground almonds, icing sugar, sweetener, corn flour, raisins and butter.

Line a cookie sheet with a sheet of greaseproof paper. Lay walnut-sized spoonfuls of the dough on it. Spread them out leaving enough room between them so that they do not stick together during cooking.

Bake the cookies for 15 minutes until golden brown.

Recommended accompaniments
Cucumbers in cream, spinach patties.

Nutrition tips
The combination of dried fruit and nuts (ground almonds) makes this dessert a good source of potassium, magnesium, calcium, vitamin E and fiber.

CINNAMON COOKIES
Morocco

👥 Makes 20 cookies   ☰ 10 mins   ◑ 20 mins

🍸 62 calories per cookie

3 egg whites
1 tablespoon ground
  cinnamon
1½ cups ground almonds

⅓ cup brown sugar
1½ tablespoons granulated
  sweetener
Salt

Preheat the oven to 350 °F.

Beat the egg whites to stiff peaks after adding a pinch of salt.

In a shallow bowl, mix together the ground almonds, cinnamon, sweetener and brown sugar. Carefully fold in the egg whites.

Cover a cookie sheet with greaseproof paper. Then, using a tablespoon or an icing bag, drop heaps of the dough the size of large nuts on to it. Bake for 20 minutes. Leave to cool before serving. These cookies can be stored for several days in a cookie tin.

Recommended accompaniments
Veal cholent, pear and apple compote.

Nutrition tips
Cinnamon is a spice and has been used as a medicinal plant for centuries. It can help soothe digestive problems.

ALMOND BROWNIES
USA

👥 16 brownies   ☰ 10 mins   ◑ 25 mins

🍸 185 calories per brownie

1¼ cups chocolate,
  70% cocoa content
1 cup ground almonds
¾ cup low-fat butter (20% fat)
⅓ cup raw sugar

1½ tablespoons granulated
  sweetener
3 eggs
½ cup white flour

Preheat the oven to 300 °F.

Break up the chocolate into a bowl. Add 2 tablespoons water and melt the chocolate in the microwave, or in a bain-marie.

In a shallow bowl, stir together the softened butter with the sugar and sweetener until the mixture froths up. Add the eggs, flour, melted chocolate and almonds.

Line a jelly roll tin (10½ inch × 8 inch) with waxed paper and turn the dough into the tin. Bake in the oven for 15 minutes.

Recommended accompaniments
Cabbage and apple salad, smoked salmon with eggs.

Nutrition tips
Chocolate is a good source of potassium, magnesium, calcium, iron and phenyllethylamine, a product similar to amphetamines with which it shares certain properties. It is however also high in fats (25 to 35%) and should therefore be consumed in moderation.

NEW YORK BROWNIES
USA

🚶 20 brownies   ≡ 15 mins   ▤ 25 mins
🍷 130 calories per brownie

¾ cup powdered cocoa
⅓ cup raw sugar
2 tablespoons granulated
   sweetener
1 egg
4 egg whites

1½ cups matzo meal
⅓ cup cornstarch
1 teaspoon vanilla extract
1 cup ground almonds
3 tablespoons sunflower oil

Preheat the oven to 300 °F.

In a shallow bowl, mix together the raw sugar, sweetener, cornstarch, eggs, vanilla, cocoa, matzo meal and ground almonds. Stir vigorously.

Turn the dough into a non-stick jelly roll tin (about 10½ inch × 8 inch) and bake in the oven for 25 minutes.

Cut into small squares while still hot. Then leave the brownies to cool before serving.

Recommended accompaniments
Beef pancakes, plain raw vegetables.

Nutrition tips
Be aware that so-called 'diet' chocolate has the same number of calories as traditional chocolate. One is lower in carbohydrates but contains more fat, while the other has a lower fat content but contains more sugar.
On average, 100g chocolate contains 550 to 600 calories.

HONEY CAKE
Poland

Serves 12   45 mins   1 hour 15 mins
130 calories per serving

¼ cup granulated sugar
1 tablespoon granulated
   sweetener
2 egg whites
1⅔ cups white flour
2 teaspoons baking powder
½ cup clear honey
Salt

1 tablespoon low-sugar
   orange marmalade
1 pinch baking soda
1 teaspoon cinnamon
7 tablespoons strong coffee
2 tablespoons ground almonds
1 tablespoon sunflower oil

Preheat the oven to 350 °F.
   In a bowl, stir the honey into the hot coffee. Leave to cool.
   In a shallow bowl, mix together the flour, coffee and honey, sugar, sweetener, marmalade, baking powder, bicarbonate of soda, cinnamon, oil and almonds.
   Whisk the eggs to stiff peaks, adding a pinch of salt. Carefully fold this into the other ingredients. Turn the dough into a non-stick cake tin. Bake for 45 minutes.

Recommended accompaniments
Romanian roast kid, vegetable kugel.

Nutrition tips
Honey is defined as a food produced by bees from the nectar of flowers or their secretions. There is also 'sugar cane honey', which is honey produced by bees that are fed on sugar.

COMPOTE OF DRIED FRUIT
Eastern Europe

🍴 Serves 6   ≡ 5 mins   ⟷ 30 mins

🍷 210 calories per serving

1 cup dried apricots
1 cup pitted prunes
⅔ cup raisins
1 teaspoon cinnamon

1 tablespoon granulated
  sweetener
Zest of 1 lemon

Rinse and drain the apricots, prunes and raisins.
    Put them in a pan and cover with cold water. Add the sweetener, cinnamon and lemon zest. Half cover the pan with a lid to prevent the fruit boiling over.
    Simmer gently for 30 minutes until the fruit is tender.
    Leave to cool, then chill the fruit in the fridge for 1 hour.
    Serve the compote for dessert in individual goblets.

Recommended accompaniments
Yogurt with paprika, zucchini with eggs.

Nutrition tips
Dried fruit is obtained from dehydrating fresh fruit. It contains the same components as fresh fruit but 4 or 5 times more concentrate, with the exception of vitamin C.
    Dried fruit is an excellent source of fiber, magnesium, iron, potassium (900 to 1,200mg per 100g) and vitamin A.
    It is, however, not recommended if you have intestinal problems.

APPLE MERINGUE
USA

Serves 8 ≡ 15 mins ⧖ 35 mins

275 calories per serving

15 Golden Delicious
  apples
1 tablespoon granulated
  sweetener
1 teaspoon lemon zest
3 egg whites

¼ cup granulated sugar
1 tablespoon lemon juice
¾ cup chopped nuts
1 teaspoon cinnamon
1 pinch salt

Preheat the oven to 300 °F.

Peel, core and cut the apples into chunks.

Put the apples in a pan together with half of the sugar, the sweetener, lemon juice, lemon zest, chopped nuts and the cinnamon. Half cover with a lid and simmer for 10 minutes, stirring occasionally.

Beat the eggs until they are stiff, after adding a pinch of salt. Add the remaining sugar and continue to beat to form stiff peaks.

Turn the compote into an oval gratin dish (about 13 inches long) and cover with the stiff egg whites. Bake in the oven for 30 minutes until the top is golden brown.

Serve this apple meringue warm.

Recommended accompaniments
Eggplant caviar, 1 × 10g matzo, stuffed tomatoes and peppers.

Nutrition tips
Apples are rich in fiber.

Nuts are a good source of Omega 3 fatty acids, vitamin E and polyphenols with antioxidant properties, as well as magnesium, potassium and copper, which improve blood pressure. For all these reasons, this is a good dessert to help prevent heart disease.

PEAR AND APPLE COMPOTE
France

👪 Serves 6   ☰ 10 mins   ⌛ 15 mins

🍷 70 calories per serving

5 Royal Gala or Golden Delicious apples	½ teaspoon cinnamon
5 pears	2 teaspoons granulated sweetener
Zest of half a lemon	

Peel and core the apples and pears, then cut them into chunks. Grate the peel of half a lemon.

Put the apple and pear chunks into a pan. Add the cinnamon, sweetener and lemon zest.

Cover with cold water and half cover with a lid to prevent the fruit boiling over.

Simmer for 15 minutes, stirring occasionally to prevent the mixture sticking.

Serve this compote warm or cold.

Recommended accompaniments
Veal cholent, 1 cinnamon cookie.

Nutrition tips
The ideal dessert for regular digestive transit!

Discovered in the United States at the beginning of the 20th century, Golden Delicious apples are available throughout the year.

APPLE AND RAISIN COMPOTE
Poland

👪 Serves 6   ☰ 10 mins   ⌛ 15 mins

🍷 100 calories per serving

6 Golden Delicious or Royal Gala apples	2 teaspoons ground cinnamon
⅓ cup raisins	1 teaspoon granulated sweetener
Zest of half a lemon	

Peel and core the apples, then cut them into chunks. Grate the peel of half a lemon.

Tip the apples into a pan together with the raisins, cinnamon, sweetener and lemon zest. Cover with cold water and half cover with a lid to stop the fruit boiling over. Simmer gently for 15 minutes, stirring occasionally. Serve this compote warm or cold.

Recommended accompaniments
Beet borscht, beef meatballs.

Nutrition tips
Raisins are rich in potassium, fiber and magnesium. They can help prevent heart disease and certain cancers. Although high in calories (300 calories per 100g), they are suitable for a weight-loss diet when combined with apples.

COUCOUS WITH YOGURT
France

🏃 Serves 4   ≡ 15 mins   ⊡ 1½ mins

🍷 160 calories per serving

This dessert can be prepared using couscous leftovers
2½ cup cooked couscous
1 cup fat-free stirred yogurt (only if your meal does not include meat)
1 teaspoon cinnamon
⅓ cup raisins
4 mint leaves
1 teaspoon granulated sweetener

Wash and drain the mint leaves. Put the raisins to swell up in a bowl of hot water for 10 minutes.

In a microwave-proof shallow bowl, mix the couscous with the cinnamon, raisins and sweetener.

Heat the mixture in the microwave for 1½ minutes on full power. Stir the yogurt thoroughly into the couscous.

Next, fill individual ramekins with this dessert. Turn the ramekins on to dessert plates to give you a half-globe. Place a mint leaf on top and serve as a dessert or main dish.

In this recipe, the yogurt can be replaced by 3 tablespoons 5% fat crème fraîche.

Recommended accompaniments
Zucchini with eggs, chachouka.

Nutrition tips
It is better to stick to yogurt rather than use crème fraîche in order to retain the amount of calcium and protein in this dish.

CHEESECAKE
USA

👪 Serves 10   ≡ 15 mins   ⌛ 1 hour 15 mins
🍷 160 calories per serving

2 eggs
1½ cups fat-free yogurt
1 cup low-fat cream cheese
3 tablespoons lemon juice
1 teaspoon vanilla extract
4 egg whites
1 cup 20% fat yogurt

½ cup low-fat cream
 (6%) cheese
⅓ cup granulated sugar
1 tablespoon granulated
 sweetener
1 teaspoon lemon zest
Salt

Preheat the oven to 350 °F.

Beat the whole eggs in a bowl. In another large bowl, whisk all the yogurt and cream cheese with an electric whisk. Add the 2 beaten eggs, lemon juice, lemon zest, the sugar and the sweetener.

Beat the 4 egg whites, salted, until they form stiff peaks. Carefully fold the egg whites into the cheese. Turn the mixture into a non-stick jelly roll tin (about 8 × 10½ × 2 inch).

In a pan, bring 4 cups water to the boil. Pour the water into an oven dish with a bigger capacity than the jelly roll tin to make a bain-marie.

Lay a sheet of waxed paper over the cheesecake mixture and bake covered in the oven for 1 hour. Take off the waxed paper and continue cooking for a further 5 minutes. Leave the cheese-cake to cool, then cut it into squares and serve.

You can serve this cheesecake with strawberry coulis.

Recommended accompaniments
Eggplant caviar, stuffed cabbage.

Nutrition tips
Note the high-protein content of this recipe (29g).

PISTACHIO FONDANT
Algeria

🐄 Serves 8   ≡ Prepare the day before, then 10 mins
🍸 180 calories per serving

1 packet of 36 ladyfingers	50g ground almonds
1 cup skim milk	50g chopped pistachios
1 tablespoon granulated	1 teaspoon vanilla powder
sweetener	or half a teaspoon natural
2 cups fat-free yogurt	vanilla extract

The day before, pour the milk and vanilla into a shallow bowl. Soak the biscuits and line the base and sides of an 7 inch diameter mold.

In a bowl, mix the pistachio nuts, almonds, sweetener and yogurt. Turn the mixture into the mold lined with soaked ladyfinger biscuits.

Chill over night in the fridge.

Next day, turn out the pistachio fondant.

Recommended accompaniments
Fish soup
    Or purée of eggplants with tomatoes, fish with paprika.

Nutrition tips
The fondant can be accompanied by unsweetened red fruit coulis served separately.

    This dessert provides 5g protein per person, or the equivalent of a serving of cheese.

BUBBELEH – PASSOVER PANCAKE
Poland

🚶 Serves 4 ≡ 10 mins ⊡ 6 mins

🍸 150 calories per serving

4 eggs	1 tablespoon sugar
2 tablespoons matzo meal	1 teaspoon granulated
2 teaspoons sunflower oil	sweetener
Salt	

Separate the egg whites from the yolks. In a shallow bowl, mix together the egg yolks, half the sugar, the sweetener and the matzo meal.

In a bowl, whisk the egg whites to form stiff peaks, after adding a pinch of salt. Fold the whites gently into the yolks, matzo meal and sugar.

Turn the mixture into a large oiled, non-stick frying pan to form a large pancake. Brown either side gently for 3 minutes each.

Lay the pancake on a large plate and cut it into 1¼ inch squares. Sprinkle with the remaining sugar and serve warm or cold, with a cup of tea, for breakfast, at teatime or for dessert at Pesach.

Because of its sweetness, this snack or dessert is called 'bubbeleh', Yiddish for 'little grandmother'.

Nutrition tips
May be eaten for breakfast. It is equivalent to 40g bread and 10g butter.

CREAMY CHEESECAKE
Poland

🚶 Serves 8 ≡ 15 mins ⊡ 1 hour

🍸 140 calories per serving

6 eggs	2 tablespoons raisins
¾ cup 20% fat cream cheese	1 tablespoon granulated
¼ cup sugar	sweetener
1 pinch vanilla powder	⅔ cup white flour
2 cups fat-free yogurt	1 pinch salt

Soak the raisins in a bowl of hot water.

In a large pan, mix together the cream cheese yogurt, flour, sweetener, sugar, vanilla and 2 whole eggs.

Preheat the oven to 350 °F.

Separate the whites from the yolks of the remaining eggs. Set aside the yolks.

In a large bowl, whisk the egg whites to stiff peaks, sprinkling with a pinch of salt. Fold them carefully into the rest of the ingredients and turn into a cake pan. Drain the raisins and scatter them over the surface of the mixture. Cover with a sheet of waxed paper.

Bake for 15 minutes at 350 °F, then for 15 minutes at 400 °F, then for 15 minutes at 350 °F, and finally for 15 minutes at 400 °F. This cooking method will stop the cake from sinking.

Once cold, cut it into rectangles.

Cheesecake is, together with apple strudel, the most popular cake among Polish and Russian Jews.

Recommended accompaniments
Carp and hake fish cakes, dressed green salad.

Or plain raw vegetables, onion soufflé, hake with carrots.

Nutrition tips
This is a high-protein dessert (12g per serving). You can use it to top up your protein intake.

HONEY CAKE
United States

🧑 Serves 12   ≡ 15 mins   ⧉ 60 mins

🍷 190 calories per serving

2 eggs	½ teaspoon cinnamon
¼ cup sugar	1 tablespoon sunflower oil
½ tablespoon granulated	1 teaspoon baking powder
sweetener	1 teaspoon bicarbonate
7 tablespoons coffee	of soda
1½ cups flour	1 pinch ground clove
1 cup chopped nuts	1 pinch ground nutmeg
⅔ cup raisins	1 pinch ginger, grated
½ cup clear honey	or ground

Preheat the oven to 350 °F.

Put the raisins to swell up in a bowl of hot water for 10 minutes. Drain.

In a shallow bowl, beat the eggs, sugar and sweetener until the mixture froths up, then add the oil.

Dilute the honey in the hot coffee, then leave to cool.

In a large bowl, mix the flour, baking powder, bicarbonate of soda, cinnamon, ginger, clove and nutmeg. Add the eggs then the honey and coffee. Stir everything together and add the nuts and raisins.

Turn the dough into a loaf pan lined with a sheet of waxed paper. Bake in the oven for 50 to 60 minutes until the cake is golden brown. Use a skewer to check whether the cake is done. If it comes out clean, the cake is ready. Leave to cool before turning the cake out of the tin.

Recommended accompaniments
Stuffed avocados, sauerkraut with pike.

Nutrition tips
The combination of dried fruit and nuts makes this dessert a good source of potassium, magnesium, calcium, vitamin E and fiber.

LEMON MOUSSE CAKE WITH POPPY SEEDS
USA

👥 Serves 12   ≡ 15 mins   ⧛ 1 hour
🍸 110 calories per serving

5 egg yolks	7 tablespoons lemon juice
2 untreated lemons	1 tablespoon granulated
¼ cup granulated sugar	sweetener
½ cup poppy seeds	1 cup matzo meal
3 tablespoons cornstarch	1 teaspoon cream of tartar
10 egg whites	Salt

Preheat the oven to 325 °F.

Immerse the poppy seeds in hot water for 3 minutes until they swell up, then drain. Grate the peel of 2 lemons. In a shallow bowl, mix together 5 egg yolks, half the sugar and the sweetener.

Whisk these ingredients to a frothy mixture. Add the lemon zest, lemon juice and poppy seeds. Add the matzo meal and corn flour.

Whisk the egg whites to stiff peaks, after adding a sprinkling of salt, the cream of tartar and the remaining sugar.

Fold the egg whites carefully into the rest of the ingredients. Turn the dough into a loaf pan lined with waxed paper.

Bake in the oven for 1 hour.

Recommended accompaniments
Raw vegetables with egg salad, stuffed mushrooms.

Nutrition tips
This is a low-calorie dessert that provides 5g protein per serving (the same as one yogurt).

ORANGE CAKE
Algeria

🏃 Serves 10   ≡ 10 mins   ⊞ 35 mins

🍷 100 calories per serving

3 eggs
¼ cup granulated sugar
1 tablespoon granulated
   sweetener
1¼ cups white flour

1 teaspoon baking powder
Zest of 2 oranges
Juice of 1 orange
Salt

Preheat the oven to 300 °F.
   Separate the egg whites from the yolks. In a shallow bowl, mix together the egg yolks with the sugar and sweetener to obtain a frothy mixture. Add the flour, orange zest and baking powder. Stir and add the orange juice.
   In a large bowl, beat the eggs to form stiff peaks, after adding a pinch of salt. Fold them carefully into the yolks.
   Turn the dough into a non-stick, high-sided cake tin.
   Bake in the oven for 35 minutes.

Recommended accompaniments
Raw vegetable salad, breaded scallops, spinach with mushrooms.
   Or raw vegetables with egg salad, beef with navy beans.

Nutrition tips
Wash the oranges thoroughly in warm water before grating them.

TEA AND DATE CAKE
Middle East

🏃 Serves 12   ≡ Prepare the day before, then 25 mins

⊞ 1 hour   🍷 200 calories per serving

1⅔ cups white flour
2 Earl Grey tea bags
1½ tablespoons granulated
   sweetener

3 cup fresh dates
⅓ cup brown sugar
1 egg
2 teaspoons baking powder

The day before, bring 1 cup water to the boil in a pan. Put the tea bags in a bowl and add the water. Steep for 15 minutes. Then, remove the tea bags and leave the tea to cool.

Stone and chop the dates. Beat the eggs in a bowl.

In a shallow bowl, mix the flour with the egg, sugar, sweetener and the tea and dates.

Cover and leave to stand over night at room temperature.

Next day, preheat the oven to 350 °F

Turn the mixture into a loaf pan lined with waxed paper. Bake in the oven for 1 hour.

Leave to cool and turn out of the tin before serving.

Recommended accompaniments
Sweet pepper salad, Moroccan chicken tagine.

Nutrition tips
Dates are a good source of calcium (71mg per 100 g, iron (2mg per 100g), vitamin B3 and fiber.

They are high in calories (300 calories per 100g) and should be consumed in moderation.

ORANGE FLOWER SPONGE CAKE
Algeria

Serves 8   ≡ 10 mins   35 mins

170 calories per serving

1 cup white flour	Salt
3 egg yolks	3 teaspoons orange flower
5 eggs	water
¼ cup sugar	2 teaspoons orange zest
1 tablespoon granulated	2 teaspoons lemon juice
sweetener	2 teaspoons baking powder

Preheat the oven to 300 °F

Separate the egg whites from the yolks.

In a shallow bowl, mix the egg yolks with the sugar and sweetener to obtain a frothy consistency. Add the flour, baking powder, orange flower water, orange zest and lemon juice. Stir thoroughly.

In a large bowl, beat the egg whites to stiff peaks, after adding a pinch of salt. Carefully fold the egg whites into the rest of the ingredients.

Turn the dough into a non-stick, high-sided cake pan.

Bake for 35 minutes.

Recommended accompaniments
Fennel salad, chachouka, beef with lemon.

Nutrition tips
Wash the oranges thoroughly in warm water before grating them.

APPLE KUGEL
Central Europe

🚶 Serves 8   ≡ 20 mins   ⌧ 45 mins

🍷 170 calories per serving

4 Golden Delicious apples	1 whole egg
4 egg whites	½ teaspoon cinnamon
6 matzo biscuits	⅓ cup raisins
½ cup ground almonds	1 orange
1 tablespoon granulated sweetener	¼ cup granulated sugar

Preheat the oven to 350 °F

Put the raisins in a bowl of hot water for 10 minutes to let them swell up.

Peel and core the apples and cut them into chunks. Crumble the matzos. Put them in a strainer, soak them in cold water and drain. Grate the orange. Then squeeze the orange flesh.

In a shallow bowl, mix the whole egg with the egg whites, 1 tablespoon sugar, the sweetener, matzos, cinnamon, raisins, ground almonds, the apples and the orange zest and juice.

Sprinkle the base of a non-stick cake pan (about 12 × 8 × 2 inch) with the remaining sugar and a pinch of cinnamon.

Turn the mixture into the pan and bake in the oven for 45 minutes.

Serve this apple kugel warm.

Recommended accompaniments
Sweet pepper salad, veal meatballs with onions.

Nutrition tips
This dessert provides 5g protein per person.
The combination of apples, almonds and raisins makes this recipe important in helping to prevent heart disease and the onset of certain cancers.

BLINIS WITH YOGURT
Russia

Serves 5   10 mins   10 mins
110 calories per serving

1 egg
1 cup yogurt
2½ tablespoons white flour

1 tablespoon granulated
   sweetener
2 teaspoons sunflower oil

In a shallow bowl, mix the egg with the yogurt and flour. To avoid lumps forming, beat with an electric whisk.

Heat an oiled, non-stick frying pan and drop tablespoonfuls of the batter into it, leaving plenty of space between them to prevent them sticking together during cooking. Brown the blinis for 2 minutes on either side.

Sprinkle with the sweetener and serve warm.

Recommended accompaniments
Smoked salmon with red fruit, stuffed tomatoes
   Or sweet pepper salad, mackerel with tomatoes.

Nutrition tips
This dessert provides 5g protein and 110 calories per person, the equivalent of one sweetened yogurt.
   Pancakes are a childhood favourite. It is important to be able to include them in a weight-loss diet.

BAKED APPLES WITH YOGURT
(or without yogurt, as a side dish to meat dishes)
Russia

Serves 6   15 mins   40 mins

110 calories per serving (with yogurt),
90 (without yogurt).

6 Golden Delicious apples	2 teaspoons granulated
1 teaspoon cinnamon	sweetener
2 cups 20% fat yogurt	2 tablespoons raisins

Preheat the oven to 350 °F.

Put the raisins to swell up in a bowl of hot water for 15 minutes. Drain the raisins. Wash and wipe the apples. Cut off the tops to give you little lids.

Remove the cores with an apple corer. In a bowl, mix the yogurt with the sweetener, cinnamon and raisins.

Fill the centres of the apples with this mixture, then put the 'lid' back on each one. Arrange them on an oven dish. Pour 2 glasses of water into the dish.

Bake the apples for 40 minutes. Serve them warm for dessert.

Recommended accompaniments
Quick beet borscht, zucchini with eggs, baked apples with yogurt.
Or beef meatballs, kasha, baked apples without yogurt.

Nutrition tips
The marriage of apples and raisins makes this a dish that can help prevent heart disease and the onset of certain cancers.

YOGURT AND RAISIN RAVIOLI
Russia

🎎 Serves 8   ≡ 30 mins   ⊡ 6 mins

🍹 140 calories per serving

1 packet of 40 samosa pastry
  sheets
1 tablespoon granulated sugar
1 teaspoon ground
  cinnamon
1 teaspoon lemon zest

2 tablespoons sunflower oil
1 cup fat-free yogurt
1 teaspoon granulated
  sweetener
⅓ cup raisins
2 egg whites

Soak the raisins for 10 minutes in a bowl of hot water. Drain the raisins.

In a shallow bowl, mix the yogurt with the raisins, sugar, sweetener, egg whites, the cinnamon and the lemon zest.

Roll out the sheets of samosa pastry. Cut circles from the pastry using a whisky glass. Place a teaspoon of filling in the centre and close up to form ravioli pillows. Press the sides down firmly. Repeat the operation until there is no filling left.

Oil a non-stick frying pan and brown the ravioli for 3 minutes on either side.

Remove excess fat with kitchen roll and sprinkle the ravioli with sugar and cinnamon.

This dessert should be served with a vegetarian meal.

Recommended accompaniments
Hake with carrots, zucchini with eggs.

Nutrition tips
This is the equivalent of one dairy product + one piece of fruit.

APPLE STRUDEL
Romania

🕵 Serves 6   ≡ 30 mins   ⧄ 40 mins

🍷 270 calories per serving

9 ounce pack unsweetened
  pastry
1 egg yolk
8 Royal Gala and Golden
  Delicious apples
¼ cup chopped nuts
2 tablespoons raisins
1 tablespoon vanilla sugar

1 teaspoon cinnamon
1 tablespoon granulated
  sweetener
1 tablespoon low-sugar jam
1 tablespoon low-sugar
  marmalade
Half a lemon

Preheat the oven to 350 °F.

In a bowl, beat the egg yolk and set aside. Squeeze the half lemon. Put the raisins in a bowl of hot water to swell up for 10 minutes. Drain the raisins. Peel, core and cut the apples into quarters then into thin slices. Set aside a third of the apples. Place the rest in a pan. Add the vanilla sugar, cover with the lid and simmer very gently for 5 minutes. Stir and make sure the apples are not sticking.

In a large bowl, mix the raw apples with the cooked apples, the jam and marmalade, the cinnamon, raisins, chopped nuts, sweetener and lemon juice.

Roll out the pastry and lay it on a cookie sheet lined with waxed paper. Pour the mixture down the middle of the sheet in a long strip. Fold in the sides of the pastry to form a long roll. Brush the surface over with egg yolk.

Bake in the oven for 40 minutes.

Recommended accompaniments

Chopped liver with chives, Russian pickled cucumbers, plain raw vegetables.

Or plain raw vegetables, chicken in broth.

Nutrition tips

The combination of apples with almonds and raisins makes this a dish that can help prevent heart disease and the onset of certain cancers.

The other courses in your meal should be low in fat but high in protein.

FOUR-FRUIT SALAD
France

🚶 Serves 4 　　≡ 10 mins

🍷 70 calories per serving

2 Comice pears	2 kiwis
4 clementines	12 white Italian grapes

Peel and core the pears. Cut them into quarters then into thin slices. Peel the clementines and kiwis and cut them into discs.

Wash, drain and remove the grapes from the stalks. Cut the grapes in half and remove the seeds.

Divide up the fruit into equal portions and arrange it attractively in four individual goblets.

Chill in the fridge for 30 minutes before serving.

Recommended accompaniments
Sweet pepper salad, veal meatballs with onions.

Nutrition tips
The ideal dessert for a weight-loss diet. It is a good source of fiber, minerals and vitamins.

SUMMER FRUIT SALAD
France

🚶 Serves 6 　　≡ 10 mins

🍷 65 calories per serving

2 cups strawberries	2 kiwis
1 cup raspberries	Half a lemon
2 white peaches	1 tablespoon granulated
2 yellow peaches	sweetener
2 apricots	6 mint leaves

Wash and drain the mint leaves. Wash, trim and cut the strawberries in half from top to bottom. Wash and drain the raspberries. Peel the peaches, cut them into quarters then into slices. Wash and drain the apricots, cut them in half then into slices. Peel and slice the kiwis. Squeeze the half lemon.

Place the fruit in a large bowl. Add the lemon juice and sweetener and stir gently.

Chill the fruit in the fridge for 1 hour before serving in individual goblets. Decorate each with a mint leaf.

Recommended accompaniments
Stuffed chicken, carrots with raisins.

Nutrition tips
To be consumed without moderation!

WINTER FRUIT SALAD
France

🏃 Serves 6   ☰ 10 mins
🍷 120 calories per serving

2 pears	6 walnuts (optional)
2 apples	2 teaspoons Rum
1 small bunch black grapes	Half a lemon
1 small bunch white grapes	1 tablespoon granulated
2 clementines	sweetener
2 kiwis	

Wash, drain and deseed the grapes.

Peel and core the apples and pears, cut them into quarters then into slices. Squeeze the half lemon. Peel the kiwis and clementines and cut them into discs.

In a large bowl, mix together the apples, pears, grapes, walnuts, kiwis, clementines, lemon juice, rum and sweetener.

Place the fruit in the fridge for 1 hour before serving in individual goblets.

Recommended accompaniments
Tomato soup, carp with paprika, 1 poppyseed cookie.

Nutrition tips
A good way to eat fruit in winter. A dessert with unquestionable nutritional benefits.

EXOTIC FRUIT SALAD
France

🏃 Serves 6   ≡ 15 mins
🍷 75 calories per serving

1 mango	3 slices of pineapple
1 small papaya	Half a lemon
2 kiwis	1 tablespoon granulated
1 small slice of water	sweetener
melon	2 teaspoons Rum

Squeeze the lemon half. Peel the water melon, remove the seeds and dice the flesh. Peel the mango, cut it in half, remove the stone and dice the flesh. Peel the papaya, cut it in half lengthwise, remove the seeds and dice. Peel and dice the pineapple. Peel the kiwis and cut them into discs.

Place the fruit in a large bowl. Add the lemon juice, sweetener and rum and stir gently.

Chill in the fridge for 1 hour before serving in individual goblets.

Recommended accompaniments
Fennel salad, beef with lemon.
Or spicy Cochin chicken, rice with lentils.

Nutrition tips
This dessert is a good source of fiber, vitamins and minerals. Pineapple is good for the digestion.

SALAD OF ORANGES WITH CINNAMON
Morocco

Serves 4 **5 mins**
75 calories per serving

4 oranges	3 teaspoons orange flower
2 teaspoons ground	water
cinnamon	1 tablespoon granulated
2 tablespoons raisins	sweetener

Put the raisins to swell up in a bowl of hot water for 15 minutes. Drain the raisins.

Peel the oranges and cut them into rounds. Place them in a large bowl.

Add the raisins, orange flower water, cinnamon and sweetener. Stir everything together and place in the fridge for 1 hour.

Serve in individual goblets.

Recommended accompaniments
Moroccan chicken tagine, chachouka, orange cake.

Nutrition tips
A low-calorie dessert and packed with vitamin C.

A WEEK OF MENUS

BETWEEN 1,200 AND 1,300 CALORIES

DAY 1

Breakfast: 40g unsweetened cereal + 1 yogurt + 100g fat-free yogurt.
Lunch: Sweet pepper salad, veal meatballs with onions, apple kugel.
Dinner: Yogurt with paprika, hake with carrots, kasha, salad of oranges with cinnamon.

DAY 2

Breakfast: 1 croissant + 200 ml skimmed milk + coffee.
Lunch: Cucumbers in cream, chachouka tart, cheesecake.
Dinner: Fennel salad, beef with lemon, rice, summer fruit salad.

DAY 3

Breakfast: 1 boiled egg + 40g bread + low-fat butter + low-fat yogurt.
Lunch: Raw vegetables, meat strudel, pear and apple compote.
Dinner: Green salad, carp and hake fishcakes, horseradish, creamy cheesecake.

DAY 4

Breakfast: 1 milk-bread roll + 200g fat-free yogurt + 100 ml unsweetened orange juice.
Lunch: Spinach with chickpeas, moussaka, exotic fruit salad.
Dinner: Raw vegetable salad, tomatoes with cheese and eggs, yogurt and raisin ravioli.

DAY 5

Breakfast: 1 bowl of 200g fat-free yogurt + 2 pieces of fruit + 1 cup of tea.

Lunch: Cucumbers in cream, fish couscous, salad of oranges with cinnamon.
Dinner: Eggplant caviar, stuffed tomatoes and peppers, apple meringue.

DAY 6
Breakfast: 3 Krisprolls + low-fat butter + 1 cup semi-skimmed milk + coffee.
Lunch: Coleslaw, chicken tagine, 1 brownie.
Dinner: Cabbage and apple salad, smoked salmon with eggs, cheesecake.

DAY 7
Breakfast: 40g bread + 2 × 30g servings low-fat cheese + ½ cup fruit juice without added sugar.
Lunch: Melon salad, Romanian roast kid, apple strudel.
Dinner: Krupnik, chopped liver with chives, four-fruit salad.

HOLIDAY MENUS

The dietician's opinion

When you are on a diet, it is important not to be left out of the party. All the recipes in these menus have therefore been kept as light as possible without making them any the less enjoyable.

Drinks have not been included in the calorie calculations. You should add 90 calories for:

- 1 glass of Champagne;
- 1 × 40 ml measure of strong alcohol (vodka, whisky, gin or rum);
- 1 × 100 ml glass of wine
- 1 × 70 ml measure of dessert wine or liqueur (Port, Muscat, etc)
- 200 ml beer.

In some cases, the calorific intake is still compatible with a low-fat diet; in others, you should compensate for the extra calories by eating low-fat protein-rich foods and drinking only herb teas and broth next day.

ROSH HASHANAH
(Jewish New Year)

Raw vegetables and egg salad
Chicken in broth
Knaidelach
Apple strudel
= 630 to 640 calories per person

Or

Chachouka
Beef with spinach
Couscous with mint
Pistachio fondant
= 820 to 830 calories per person

Nutrition tips
This can be part of a diet if you treat it as your day off for the week. If you add alcohol, you should then compensate the next day by drinking only broth and herb teas and eating 0% fat dairy products, steamed vegetables and low-fat protein-rich foods (white chicken, fish, etc).

YOM KIPPUR
(Day of Atonement)

Rosh Hashanah is followed eight days later by Yom Kippur, the Day of Atonement. This is a day of fasting and abstinence when people atone and ask for forgiveness. Fasting lasts from the evening of the previous day until sundown next day. After the fast, the family comes together for a good dinner.

Coleslaw
Carp and hake fish cakes
Kreplech
Honey cake
= *830 to 840 calories per person*

Or

Sweet pepper salad
Moroccan chicken
Couscous with herbs
Orange cake
= *610 calories per person*

Nutrition tips
These are the only calories you will have all day. The meals are therefore entirely compatible with a weight-loss diet.

SHABBAT

Shabbat is the weekly rest day. From sundown on Friday until Saturday evening, no work is done including cooking, and all food must have been cooked the day before.

Chopped liver
Beef with navy beans
Apple and raisin compote
= *700 calories per person*

Or

Beef with spinach
Tabouleh
Raisin cookie
= *700 calories per person*

Nutrition tips

Shabbat can be the day off in the week, or you could limit breakfast to low-fat dairy products and lunch to steamed vegetables and a low-fat protein dish (chicken breast or fish).

SUKKOT
(Feast of Tabernacles)

Sukkot commemorates God's protection during the forty years of exodus in the desert. For this holiday, families make outdoor huts of leaves and branches and eat their meals in them for seven days. The meals symbolise abundance.

Herrings with apples
Stuffed chicken
Kahsa
New York brownie
= *750 calories per person*

Or

Spinach with chickpeas
Moussaka
Stuffed tomatoes
Cinnamon cookies
= *630 calories per person*

Nutrition tips

You can either treat this as a day off, or you can limit breakfast to low-fat dairy products and lunch to steamed vegetables and a low-fat protein dish (chicken breast or fish).

CHANUKAH
(Festival of Lights)

Chanukah commemorates the victory of the Maccabees over the Syrian troops of Antiochus (between 165 and 167 BC). The festival recalls the miracle of the oil lamp which burnt for 8 days in the Temple. To mark the holiday, one candle is lit on the first day, two on the second, and so on until the eight days are up.

Traditionally, children are given presents.

Cabbage and apple salad
Beef meatballs with onions
Latkes (potato cakes)
Winter fruit salad
= 680 *calories per person*

Or

Eggplant caviar
Spicy Cochin chicken
Rice with lentils
Exotic fruit salad
= 520 *to* 530 *calories per person*

Nutrition tips
You can either treat this as a day off, or you can limit breakfast to low-fat dairy products and lunch to steamed vegetables and a low-fat protein dish (chicken breast or fish).

PURIM
(Festival of Lots)

This festival marks the end of winter. It recalls how, in the 6th century BC, Queen Esther saved the Jews from being massacred on the orders of the Minister Haman, by appealing to King Ahasuerus on their behalf.

Mushroom and egg pâté
Beef pancakes
Poppyseed cookies
= 540 *calories per person*

Or

Raw vegetable salad
Tuna roll
Stuffed tomatoes
Tea and date cake
= *530 calories per person*

Nutrition tips
This meal is ideal for a weight-loss diet. If you add alcohol, you
should treat it as a day off.

PESACH/PASSOVER

Pesach celebrates the return of spring and commemorates the
flight of the Jews out of Egypt into the desert. For eight days, all
food involving leaven is forbidden: bread, yeast and beer. Bread
is replaced by unleavened bread.

Raw vegetables and egg salad
Carp and hake fish cakes
Chicken in broth
Passover pancake
= *740 to 750 calories per person*

Fennel salad
Pesach lamb
Tabouleh
Cinnamon cookies
= *900 calories per person*

Nutrition tips
This can be part of a diet if you treat it as your day off for the
week. If you add alcohol, you should then compensate the next
day by drinking only broth and herb teas and eating 0% fat dairy
products, steamed vegetables and low-fat protein-rich foods
(chicken breast, fish, etc).

SHAVUOT
(Pentecost)

Shavuot in the spring commemorates the ceremony of Bikkurim, or first fruits. No meat or wine is consumed during this festival, and there are plentiful dairy-based dishes instead.

Cucumbers in cream
Rapid Russian borscht
Smoked salmon with eggs
Creamy cheesecake
= *430 calories per person*

Or

Radishes with cream cheese
Chachouka
Sardines with tomatoes
Blinis with yogurt
= *560 calories per person*

Nutrition tips
Without alcohol, these meals are suitable for a weight-loss diet; with alcohol, they should be treated as a day off, or else the next meal should be adapted to consist of steamed vegetables and a low-fat protein-based food.

PART III

WEIGHT-LOSS DIET

by Annick Champetier de Ribes
Director of Dietetics at the Hôpital du Perpétual-Secours

INTRODUCTION

Jewish cookery has a very bad reputation from the nutritional point of view, and I must confess that I shared these prejudices. Getting to know Sylvie Jouffa allowed me to analyse each of her recipes, and I was interested to find that many dishes were compatible with a weight-loss diet.

In some recipes, we were able to reduce the fat with no loss of flavor.

Other recipes were impossible to change without jeopardising the flavor and we therefore decided to organise the other meals on that day around this dish.

MY WEIGHT-LOSS DIET

Every year, a new diet comes on to the market, boosted by business and the media. This has not stopped the population getting fatter.

From miracle cures to miracle recipes, people are determined to believe in magic and are ready to take all sorts of risks to shed excess weight once and for all. They hope to find the trick, the recipe that will enable them to regain their adolescent figure effortlessly.

It is like coming up with a training programme to turn an amateur sportsman into a professional champion in a month and maintain this level thereafter.

All these diets are based on a guiding principle: cut out potatoes; stick to protein; drink cabbage soup; split up foodstuffs; cut out carbohydrates; eat only raw food; follow strict menus for two weeks or more; stick to one food group per day, etc. Why are there so many failures? Precisely because there is no *one* sliming method, but a series of scientifically recognised rules that are useless if they are applied separately – as is often the case with 'miracle' diets.

Dietetics is a science that depends on an understanding of food and the human physiology. Any diet not based on scientific knowledge should be regarded with suspicion.

So, what should we keep in?

My 'diet' if it has to be defined as such, is based on understanding food, the physiology of digestion, the constraints of what food is available and cultural habits. It is designed to enable everyone to rediscover the pleasures of eating by adapting gastronomy to their daily diet.

1. Reconcile yourself to food

All of us have preconceived ideas about what foods are fattening or slimming.

There are people who think that pasta dishes are not fattening; that rice helps you lose weight; red meat is fattening; pineapple dissolves fats; fruit is fattening (or, on the contrary, slimming); cheese is fattening; bread should be cut out, or else prioritised, and so on. Should you drink with food or in between meals, should you drink or not? Should you cut out salt or not?

Are dairy products easy or difficult to digest, are they a source of calcium or likely to reduce calcium levels? And what about eggs? Is cholesterol good or bad for the liver?

All these opinions are the result of faddish diets that prove everything and its opposite. The result is the increasing dumbing-down of dietetics. The most basic rules passed down by generations of mothers have been forgotten.

The first thing you need to understand what you should eat is an *understanding of the different foods* together with some knowledge of what the different elements contribute separately and an idea of the nutritional contents of basic recipes.

My diet thus consists in going over the essential foods that answer our protein, vitamin and mineral requirements. If you are going to lose weight, you need to concentrate on *what you should eat and not what you should not eat.*

With this new knowledge, food will cease to be an irresistible temptress with a fiendish capacity for inciting gluttony. Everyone will be able to take the upper hand and enjoy cooking with equivalent foods to control their weight.

Using a *food handbook* is vital. It is a good way of knowing the facts of your intake.

Deviations are more limited because they are part of reality. In the light of the handbook, I insist, for instance, on the negative effects of a diet that supplies insufficient protein or fiber, while I am more tolerant about extra desserts. During consultations, I thus pass on nutritional knowledge that is completely tailored to each person's needs. Changes to eating habits should be made over time. This enables a diet to be better accepted and adopted long-term.

2. Understand your weight variations.

When you stand on the scales, you are weighing four elements: bones, water, fat and muscle. You need to know that any rapid variation in your visible weight on the scales over two or three days is mainly the result of loss or gain of water, especially in women after a salty or alcoholic meal.

Slimming is not only about losing weight; above all, it is a question of losing fat while retaining muscle. If the opposite happens, you will automatically put back on all the weight you lost and become discouraged.

Our bodies behave like bankers. There are current outgoings and there are reserves. *Outgoings* are calculated in calories. Some outgoings are linked to the functioning of our organs and others to physical activity. Apart from pathological situations, *our outgoings are proportional to the amount of muscle we have.* Men can eat more than women because they have more muscle. They thus have higher basic outgoings.

When people lose weight quickly and unrealistically, they stand to lose a significant amount of muscle. Their outgoings are then reduced, and they are virtually obliged to put weight back on once they go back to their normal diet.

There are two types of *reserve*: fat, which contributes calories when it deteriorates, and muscle, which brings protein to the body.

When muscle is reduced, the peripheral water increases and cellulite appears. When your intake exceeds your needs, the surplus energy is stored in the fatty tissue.

When your intake is lower than your outgoings, the calories are taken from your reserves, either those stored in fatty tissue or those stored in muscle.

In most fashionable diets including high-protein diets, there is a considerable risk of loss of muscle for two reasons:
- either the diet is too low in protein
- or the diet is too low in calories; the protein from the food is poorly used and cannot keep up the muscle-matter.

3. How to use up fat

- Make sure you have enough protein:
  Protein is found in meat, fish, eggs and dairy products.

  In order not to lose muscle, you need to eat meat, fish or eggs once or twice a day, and three or four dairy products a day.

  Jewish tradition prohibits the consumption of milk and meat at the same meal. It is therefore essential to eat one, possibly two dairy products at breakfast.
- Vary your diet:
  For the proteins to play their part, the body must have a certain amount of carbohydrates and 'essential' fatty acids found in oils at its disposal.
- Take regular physical exercise:
  Make exercise part of your daily life: go for a walk; walk upstairs; control the position of your back and stomach. Take up a sport: swimming, cycling, the local gym, physical exercises at home, and so on.

4. Don't eat between meals

During meals, the body stores calories. Between meals, the fats are used. Any nibbling, whether of solids or liquids, slows down or stops the need to take from the reserves.

Some diets are based on eating lots of meals to increase outgoings. This method is actually used to help people put on weight!

Other diets advise eating fruit between meals, either to improve digestion or to interrupt the afternoon. Remember that the physiology of the digestive tube is adapted to three meals a day after the age of 18, and that snacks and teatime are only recommended for children, adolescents, pregnant and nursing women and old people. Nibbling and snacking often involve carbohydrates. They are responsible for a dietary imbalance and induce a feeling of hunger between meals, which leads to a change in eating habits.

5. Know and respect your requirements

If you restrict your diet too much, you will always lack vitamins and oligo-elements such as iron. This can cause fatigue, anaemia, anxiety and depression.

• *Calorie rate*
How much energy you expend will depend on your age, sex, height, weight and percentage of muscle.
The Harris Benedict equation is used to calculate the basal energy expenditure (B.E.E.):

$$B.E.E. = 66.743 + (13.752 \times W. + 5.003 \times H. - 6.755 \times A.)$$
in men
$$B.E.E. = 655.096 + (9.562 \times W. + 1.850 \times H - 4.676 \times A)$$
in women

W. = weight in kilos   A. = age in years
H. = height in cm   The B.E.E. is expressed in calories.

Including the expenditure involved in physical activity, the true needs are 20 to 30% more than the basal energy expenditure. The ideal calorie rate needed to lose weight without risk is therefore equal to the B.E.E.

• *The division of nutrients must be balanced*
To deal with this expenditure, energy is provided by food according to three classes of nutrients: protein, fats and carbohydrates.
Energy is expressed in kilocalories (Kcal).
1 Kcal = 4.18 kilojoules (international unit).

1g fat releases 9 Kcal (38 Kj).
1g carbohydrates releases 4 Kcal (17 Kj).
1g protein releases 4 Kcal (17 Kj).

Fats

Fats should represent 30 to 35% of the total kilocalories, or 75g for a daily ration of 2,000 calories. They occur naturally in a variety of elements:

- *Visible animal fats*: butter, cream, beef suet, veal fat, meat fat. They are often used in processed food.
- *Invisible animal fats* contained in dairy products, meat, fish, eggs and processed food.
- *Visible vegetable fats*: oils and vegetable margarine.
- *Invisible vegetable fats*: avocado, nuts, olives, processed food.

In terms of quantity, note that all oils contain 100% fat. Butter and margarine both contain 84% fat.

In terms of quality, on the other hand, saturated fats (butter or meat, for example), which, if consumed to excess, can increase the risk of heart disease, should be distinguished from unsaturated fats that are rich in Omega 3 (fish, sunflower oil, corn oil and rape, grape seed and soya oil, as well as goose fat and margarines based on these oils), which can be beneficial for a healthy heart.

As a general rule, no food is 'bad'. Each class of fatty foods has a role to play, in terms of both nutrition and gastronomy. It is possible to stick to the cooking instructions for a given dish to bring out the flavor and balance the rest of the meal by accounting for the fat content of the main dish. It is always possible to combine gastronomy with a diet. It is a question of technique.

Carbohydrates

Carbohydrates should represent 50 to 55% of the total kilocalories, or 250g for a daily ration of 2,000 calories.

- *Added sugar*: sugar, sugary processed food, honey, jam, sweets, chocolate, soft drinks... The calorie contribution from added sugar should not exceed 10% of the total calories. This represents 50g sugar for a daily ration of 2,000 calories, i.e., 10g for your morning drink + 30g jam + 10g in a dairy product. Bad habits should be rooted out: soft (fizzy) drinks, sweet desserts, ices, snacking between meals.
- *Simple sugars in fruit*: fruit is an excellent source of vitamins, minerals and fiber. It may be eaten during meals, contrary to erroneous but all too common ideas.
- *Complex slow-release sugars (bread, starch, pulses)*: in recent years, consumption of slow sugars has significantly decreased, to the benefit of simple sugars and fats. It is important to

realise that bread, starch and pulses also contain protein, vitamins and minerals and almost no fat. If you eat them as part of a weight-loss diet, you will feel fuller sooner and be less inclined to snack between meals. Pulses and wholegrain cereals have the additional benefit of reducing the absorption of cholesterol and simple sugars.

Protein

Protein should represent 12 to 15% of your total calories, or 70g for a daily ration of 2,000 calories. They are essential for rebuilding cells and maintaining muscle. They divide into:
- animal-based protein: meat, fish, eggs and dairy products.
- vegetable-based protein: grains, pulses, bread.

Protein consists of amino acids some of which are essential, and it is therefore vital that your diet supplies your body with enough of them. Vegetable and animal protein are both necessary for their different components.

- *Make sure you have enough minerals and vitamins*

Minerals

There are no calories in minerals. They all have a specific function that make them essential to the body. The main minerals are:
- calcium: this is the main constituent of the bone matrix. It is also important in muscle contraction. Calcium and phosphorus are found in milk and dairy products.
- iron: found in red blood cells and necessary for oxygen to be transported throughout the body. The iron content in animal-based foods (meat, fish or eggs) is better absorbed than the iron in vegetable-based foods (pulses and vegetables). Too little iron in the body can cause tiredness and anaemia and make you more susceptible to infection.

Vitamins

Like minerals, vitamins act in a specific way, and vitamin deficiencies can cause disease. Lack of vitamin D, for instance, causes rickets in children and osteomalacia in adults.

There is a difference between liposoluble vitamins that are soluble in fats (A, D, E and K), and hydrosoluble vitamins, which are soluble in water (C and B).

They do not provide any calories.

- Vitamin A promotes night vision, healthy skin and growth. It is found essentially in liver, whole milk, butter and eggs. Provitamin A is contained in carrots and apricots.
- Vitamin D is essential for the absorption of calcium. It is found essentially in butter, whole-milk dairy products and eggs. It is also synthesised by the skin in sunlight.
- B group vitamins are important for the nervous system and the skin. They help the assimilation of carbohydrates. They are found essentially in grains, meat and offal.
- Vitamin C protects the body from infection. It helps iron to be absorbed. It is found essentially in raw fruit and vegetables.

- *Make sure you drink enough water and electrolytes.*

Water

The body contains 50 to 60% water. It is estimated that 1 ml water is needed for 1 calorie.

Thus, a woman whose daily requirements are estimated at 2,000 calories needs 2 litres: 1 litre from food, and 1 litre from various drinks.

Sodium (Sodium chloride = salt)

Salt acts in the distribution and regulation of water between the intra- and extra-cellular compartments. It is widely found in food and should be consumed in moderation. It is important to emphasise that restricting your sodium intake will not help you lose weight and can be dangerous.

• *Know the importance of fiber*
Fiber is beneficial for digestive transit. It increases the weight of stools by retaining intestinal water.

There is *soluble fiber* (vegetables, fruit and oat bran), involved principally in hydrating stools and in the carbohydrate and cholesterol metabolism, and *insoluble fiber* (wheat bran, almonds, dates, pulses and pineapple), whose main function is to regulate digestive transit.

A regular fiber intake can help prevent cancer of the colon.

A balanced diet should include a dish of cooked green vegetables per day and at least one raw vegetable per meal.

• *Distribute foods throughout the day*
To enjoy a balanced meal, you don't have to eliminate fatty foods or eat steamed vegetables; you just need to know how to combine dishes.

Milk and dairy products

• *Definition:* milk, yogurt, cheese, Quark and yogurt, milk-based desserts.
• *Nutritional content:* animal-based protein, saturated fats, calcium, B group vitamins, vitamins A and D.
• *Frequency:* 3 to 4 dairy products daily. To avoid eating meat and dairy products at the same meal, you should eat two dairy products at breakfast time.

Meat, fish, eggs

• *Definition:* frozen or tinned meat, offal, fresh, frozen or tinned fish, eggs.
• *Nutritional content:* animal protein, fats, iron, B group vitamins, vitamin A.
• *Frequency:* twice a day as part of a weight-loss diet, in order cover your protein and iron requirements.

Fruit and vegetables

• *Definition:* all fresh, frozen or tinned vegetables and fruit.

- *Nutritional content*: fiber, carbohydrates, vitamin C, potassium.
- *Frequency*: it is essential to eat one piece of raw fruit or a raw vegetable, or both, with every meal. One dish of cooked vegetables per day.

Bread and starch

- *Definition*: pasta, rice, couscous, pulses (lentils, chickpeas, beans, coconut, sweetcorn), potatoes, grains, bread and crispbread.
- *Nutritional content*: complex carbohydrates, vegetable protein, B group vitamins.
- *Frequency*: in a weight-loss diet, you should only have one item from this category per meal.

Fat

- *Definition*: butter, oil, crème fraîche, margarine, coconut oil.
- *Nutritional content*: fats, essential fatty acids, liposoluble vitamins (A, D, E and K).
- *Distribution*: one tablespoon oil and 10g butter are the daily minimum recommended quantities to avoid a deficiency.

Drinks

- *Definition*: only water is essential to the body.
- You are recommended to drink 1 to 2 litres per day.
- Soft drinks are not part of a weight-loss diet. You should learn to avoid 'light' drinks, as they foster a sweet tooth and will get you out of the good habit of drinking plain water. This is especially true in passing on sensible eating habits to children.
- You may drink alcohol from time to time; no more than 1 unit per meal.

- *Stick to three meals a day*

A day's food should be spread over three meals that are sufficiently nutritious to stop you having to snack. The golden rule is never to eat between meals.

Breakfast

Breakfast should cover 25% of your daily requirements. It usually includes a drink, a source of carbohydrate, a source of protein and an item containing fat.

It should be treated as a proper meal and can be varied throughout the week.

For those of you who cannot bear the idea of eating first thing, you should be aware that, from a physiological point of view, the morning is the time when your requirements are greatest. You may find that all you have to do is alter your routine to discover the pleasures of this first meal. You could, for instance, change the time you get up, lay the table the night before, vary your breakfast foods, and so on.

Studies have shown that the energy value of breakfast and teatime are in inverse proportion to body weight. In other words, children eat less than adults at breakfast and more in the evening.

Skipping breakfast makes a sensible diet impossible.

Breakfast and dinner

These two meals not only supply the body with all its nutritional requirements but also provide an essential moment of relaxation. They should be proper, sit-down meals devoted exclusively to the business of eating, with neither books nor television. It is a time for conversation and getting together with family and friends, and it represents valuable 'time out' that is important for mental balance.

Teatime is only necessary for children, adolescents, the elderly and pregnant or nursing women. Teatime snacks should be based on dairy products.

• *Learn to use equivalents*
Equivalent foods give you infinite ways of varying your diet. All you need to do is replace one equivalent element with the same type suggested in the following list.

Protein equivalents

You can replace 100g meat with:
100g boned chicken leg.
85g roast meat: chicken, guinea fowl, shoulder of lamb, roast
  veal, beef, young turkey (cooked weight).
100g fish.
60g smoked salmon.
2 eggs.
100g surimi.
300g × 20% fat yogurt.
90g tofu.
One small can of tuna or salmon in water, sardines, mackerel.

You can replace 100g 0 – 10% fat yogurt by:
2 plain or low-fat yogurts
200 ml skimmed milk.

You can replace 30g 45% fat cheese with:
200g plain low-fat yogurt.
150g × 20% fat plain yogurt.
100g × 40% fat yogurt.
2 plain or fruit yogurts.
1 whole milk yogurt.
2 × 60g yogurt, 20% fat.
200 ml semi-skimmed milk.
60g low-fat cheese.
1 egg.
1 thin slice cold meat (50g).

Carbohydrate equivalents

100g potatoes can be replaced by:
25g uncooked rice, or 100g cooked rice (3 tablespoons).
25g pasta, or 100g cooked pasta (4 tablespoons).
25g flour.
30g uncooked couscous, or 100g cooked (4 tablespoons).
35g pulses (chickpeas, lentils, kidney or navy beans), or 100g
  when cooked.

100g sweetcorn
120g mashed potato.
40g bread or 3 rusks.
100g plain chestnuts.
100g Jerusalem artichokes.
100g exotic vegetables: sweet potatoes, fresh yam, plantains.

40g bread can be replaced with:
3 rusks or 3 Swedish crispbreads.
4 rice cakes or 50g matzo.
4 crackerbreads.
2 Wasa crispbreads.
2 slices of toast.
30g unsweetened grain, such as cornflakes or oats.
1 thin pancake without sugar, or 1 blini.
30g rice, couscous or tapioca, cooked in the milk allowance
   and without sugar.
100g banana.

One fruit is equal to:
3 apricots, 1/8 pineapple, 2 kiwis, 2 small peaches, 2
   nectarines.
1 pear, 1 apple, 1 guava, 1 papaya, 1 Sharon fruit, ½ mango, 4
   plums.
2 mandarins, 1 orange, ½ grapefruit, 1 lemon, 200g
   strawberries or raspberries.
½ small melon, 1/8 watermelon, 300g blueberries, rhubarb or
   redcurrants.
1 bunch grapes (75g), ½ banana, 1 fig, 1 small handful cherries
   (10 to 15), 8
lychee, 4 greengages, ½ pomegranate.
25g dried fruit (raisins, 2 prunes, 1 fig, 2 dates, 4 dried
   apricots).
15g nuts (2 walnuts, 4 hazelnuts or almonds).
100 ml grape, pear or apricot juice.
200 ml citrus fruit juice without added sugar.

Fat equivalents

10g fat is equal to:
10g butter or margarine (a knob).
10g oil (one tablespoon).
30g crème fraîche (a tablespoon).

In the range of low-fat products, 5g fat can be replaced by:
10g light butter.
10g low-fat margarine.
30g × 15% fat crème fraîche.
40g × 10% fat salad dressing (4 tablespoons).
20g × 25% fat vinaigrette (2 tablespoons).
10g low-fat mayonnaise (1 teaspoon).

Bear in mind that most dressings, such as you would be served in a restaurant, for example, contain 1 tablespoon oil or its equivalent per starter or serving of vegetables.

Calorie equivalents

10g fat are equal to:
40g bread.
1 glass of wine (100 ml).
1 glass of Champagne.
1 × 40 ml measure strong, unsweetened alcohol (whisky, gin, vodka, rum).
1 × 70 ml measure dessert wine or liqueur (Port, Muscat).
200 ml beer or cider
½ plain avocado

Other calorie equivalents

40g bread + 10g butter = 1 croissant = 1 milk-bread roll = 1 brioche.
1 sandwich = 1 double hamburger = 1 savory pastry served as a main course (a piece of quiche or pie) = 80g bread + the equivalent of 50g meat + 15g fat.

6. Develop lasting habits

You should be able to:
- enjoy the different flavors, because this will help you feel full sooner;
- incorporate your routines and habits, because if you make a superficial change, it never lasts;
- be imaginative with your menus to avoid boredom.

The day off

Weight-loss diets often focus on food restrictions. They provide lists of forbidden foods and quantities not to be exceeded, and you are always reminded that *any deviation from the diet eliminates the benefits of the week's work.*

Effort and perseverance are supposed to be the key to success. Any 'weakness' therefore creates a sense of guilt and loss of self-worth, which is why so many diets are abandoned.

I think it is important to give yourself one day off a week as a way of making your diet more compatible with normal social life and allowing you to have the odd treat. It will stop you getting into an excessive pattern and help you establish a routine that involves a few dietary changes. It does not cancel the benefits of the week's work in the slightest.

How to compensate

If you break your diet on days other than the day off, you should make sure you prioritise protein for a couple of days and drink lots of water and herbal teas. You could also schedule into your diary a session or two of exercise.